TALES OF FIFTH AVENUE
THROUGH TIME

FRANK MUZZY

America Through Time is an imprint of Fonthill Media LLC
www.through-time.com
office@through-time.com

Published by Arcadia Publishing by arrangement with Fonthill Media LLC
For all general information, please contact Arcadia Publishing:
Telephone: 843-853-2070
Fax: 843-853-0044
E-mail: sales@arcadiapublishing.com
For customer service and orders:
Toll-Free 1-888-313-2665

www.arcadiapublishing.com

First published 2022

Copyright © Frank Muzzy 2022

ISBN 978-1-63499-418-7

All rights reserved. No part of this publication may be reproduced, stored in a retrieval system or transmitted in any form or by any means, electronic, mechanical, photocopying, recording or otherwise, without prior permission in writing from Fonthill Media LLC

Typeset in Mrs Eaves XL Serif Narrow
Printed and bound in England

Introduction

Tales of Fifth Avenue Through Time tells the tales of that dirt road in 1824 up to today through archival panoramas and yellowed photos along with current comparative images, offering a clear picture of transitions in time. Urban detectives will spot the building matches akin to the ever-popular *Tales of Manhattan Through Time*.

Tales of Fifth Avenue is the path of celebratory parades, cultures, and heroes, lest we forget that its ♪ in your Easter bonnet ♪. The avenue divides east and west Manhattan addresses: odd and even until Central Park, where the Eastside numbers mix.

It is a journey—a walk, if you will, up Fifth past the opulent mansions with their cast of character intrigues, an avenue of realized affluence of the wealthiest citizens of this new country, marketing America from its every mapped corner, showing the railroads, gold, silver, and copper mining, steamships, and the wheeling and dealing of its real estate. Death and no taxes: *Tales of Fifth Avenue Through Time* is the leading designer of so many of those mansions, Stanford White, being murdered in a rooftop theatre of his just competed Madison Square Garden by a prominent member of Fifth Avenue society over a dalliance with his teenaged bride, his anger fueled by her modeling for the nude statue affixed to the garden's roof.

Tales of Fifth Avenue is also the many that sailed on the ill-fated *Titanic* while their Fifth Avenue neighbor and fellow social club member, Bruce Ismay, chairman and director of the White Star Line, abandoned their doom in a woman-and-children-only lifeboat reportedly disguised via a head schmatta.

It is both the philanthropy and snobbery among the very rich, where their daughters would marry socially significant, albeit poor, European royalty and their sons, showgirls.

It is Mrs. Astor's society—the Four Hundred—the number of those that could fit in the new ballroom of her home, eventually razed for the Empire State Building, and society's "gay walkers," who would escort the prominent single ladies. But then it is spinster daughters that never leave those mansions and bequeath them to their dogs.

Nude figure of Evelyn Nesbit, warehoused to be placed atop Madison Square Garden.

It is the latest in fashion in the nineteenth and twentieth century crafted by tailors and dressmakers as well the latest trend, "ready to wear." It is pioneering in silent film distribution and the place to buy what every Fifth Avenue mansion needed—a grand piano, to tickle the ivories.

It is the city water reservoir becoming the reservoir of knowledge—the New York Public Library, while Andrew Carnegie donated 2,500 libraries across America.

It is Tiffany's, Harry Winston's (one-time owner of the Hope Diamond), Black Starr & Frost's, "♪Diamonds are a Girl's Best Friend♪," and Cartier, which acquired its mansion/store by a trade of a string of perils. It is also the only avenue lending its moniker to a popular candy bar.

It is the first electric sign—a giant pickle cast a green glow on the neighboring gas-lit apartments replaced by the Flatiron declaring "23 skidoo" where across the street, back in 1852, had been a main stagecoach stop along a once Native American trail through the island forest, now called Broadway.

Tales of Fifth Avenue Through Time is Thomas Edison, Mark Twain, Buffalo Bill Cody, Lilly Langtry, Pres. Ulysses S. Grant, Georgia O'Keeffe, Mary Tyler Moore, Stella Adler, and brewery man Jake Ruppert, the owner of the NY Yankees. It is tobacco heiress Doris Duke and her *nouveau-riche* butler and the sewing machine king spreading his "singer-seed" all over Fifth Avenue, producing at least twenty-four children.

It is Flo Ziegfeld and his fabulous "Ziegfeld Follies"; always the PR man, Ziggy would promote Fanny Brice, Will Rodgers, and Eddie Cantor, not to mention the publicity generated from the daily Fifth Avenue hotel milk baths for his wife, Anna Held, and not paying her milk bill because "the milk wasn't fresh enough."

Tales of Fifth Avenue is the Astors, the JP Morgans, the Guggenheims, the Rothschilds, and the Vanderbilts; the latter with their largest house in New York, among their ten-plus others on Fifth. It is a family feud with neighboring mansions, then hotels that then merged—the Waldorf-Astoria—soon to be replaced by the tallest building in the world. It is also the hotel fire no one noticed during the St. Patrick Day Parade in 1899, until those screaming guests came plummeting down on the parade below.

Tales of Fifth Avenue is 30 Rock and Museum Mile: Metropolitan Arts, the Guggenheim, the Lenox Library, the Jewish Cultural, and the Museum of the City of New York.

It is Delmonico's for steak and Café Martin to be seen, along with the avenue of crooked and otherwise politicians as well as the murderer of the son of Francis Scott Keys, Daniel Edgar Sickles, jealous of his wife's affair concurrent with his introducing his mistress to Queen Victoria.

It is the mansions built to last 100 years giving new meaning to being "razed on Fifth Avenue" when they were replaced for high rises in less than twenty years, while millionaires resisting, but giving in to profits. It is the churches for the mansions that remain now surrounded by those high-rises.

Fifth Avenue was the temporary home of the torch segment of the Statue of Liberty, where to raise funds for the base, a contribution of 50 cents was requested.

Two double-decker Fifth Avenue buses turn around in Washington Square, awaiting passengers.

It was also home to the numerous triumphal arches, one at the beginning of Fifth Avenue, an unofficial monument for the 10,000-plus yellow fever victims still buried beneath Washington Square.

It is Central Park being planned after an 1840s Thursday evening's tradition of the all-male millionaires (today, billionaires) socials in the Robert Minturn home, when his wife, party crashing, suggested, "Wouldn't it be nice to plan a park as a lovely place for the wealthy to stroll and ride carriages through while providing a healthy environment for the 'poor'?" Hastening the project was the fact that Robert owned and would donate much of the land that would become "Central Park." It is the other 59th Street bridge, the literary walk, and the Bethesda fountain with the *Angel of the Waters*, her healing waters, doing her best during the AIDS epidemic. Let us not forget the Zoo and disregard the mansion complaints about "zoo smells." Hell's Bells, it is 1911—a nickel lets us take the double decker autobus up Fifth Avenue.

FIFTH & 7TH: The Washington Square Arch, looking through the arch at the beginning of Fifth Avenue in 1901. The development of Fifth Avenue by Henry Brevoort in 1834 on his multi-generational land stretching, since 1701, from the Bowery up to 14th Street began when he convinced his son, Henry, Jr., to build his mansion along a still unpaved road, northwest corner at no. 24 Fifth Avenue—purposely to generate a row of mansions to become the wealthiest neighborhood in the city, away from the smells and corruption of the immigrant's "5 points section" and the waterfront. Ten years before, it had been the gentrification of a sordid past of a potter's field into Washington Square and by 1828, George Rogers would build his country home facing the northern end of the new park. He simply ignored that it was filled with the graves of over 20,000 poor people and yellow fever victim's tombs as well as those hanged from segregated hanging trees and internment on the southern hem. Manhattan's then first families—the Minturns, the Grinnells, and apparently the Rogers—did not mind reported ghost sightings hanging from those trees. In true *Poltergeist* tradition: "But they left the bodies."

FIFTH & E 8TH: Heading north across Washington Square, past the arch, and up Fifth Avenue, the first house on the right (1), at no. 1 Fifth Avenue, remaining today (see p. 5) was the home of William Butler Duncan (2), banker and RR executive, whose frequent guests included the prince of Wales (3), son of Queen Victoria, and soon to be King Edward VII of England (1901–1910). Two mansions further at no. 5 was the home of Charles F. Chickering, as the Chickering's piano showroom (4) was at Fifth and 18th. The corner at no. 7 was the upscale "Russell" Apartments, while just across 8th Street, built by the land holding Brevoort family in 1845, the Brevoort Hotel remained there for more than a century. In 1954, it was demolished (5, *photo by James Kavallines, from the Greenwich Village Society for Historical Preservation*). The last mansion at no. 19 was the home of Dr. Edward L. Partridge (6), known as a prominent physician and devoted preservationist of the Hudson River Valley. Below, today, the apartment house at no. 11 that replaced the demolished "Borvoort" (image left) honors its predecessor by retaining the name, but the high rise that replaced the "Russell" adopted the designation "One Fifth Avenue." It caused controversy in 1927—a twenty-seven-story building (photo right) among the brownstones.

FIFTH & W 8TH ENTWINEMENT: Mary Rogers Rhinelander, inheriting the corner lot from her father, John Rogers, built the lot's first mansion (1) in 1840 at no. 2, with the entrance facing the park at no. 14 Washington Square. The home became the repository of the wealthy family's art collections and, over the next eighty years, notable for entertaining including a reception for Sarah Bernhardt (2) in 1916. The Rhinelander's daughter, Mary, would wed their neighbor, Lispenard Stewart, of no. 6 Fifth Avenue. The Stewart's son, Senator Lispenard Stewart (4), was named the most eligible bachelor, albeit confirmed, in New York in 1890. Perhaps predictably, he was also noted as the best dancer in Newport and escorted Gertrude Vanderbilt (5) to her coming-out party. Entwining the block further, the Stewart's daughter would then wed the neighbor in between at no. 4 Fifth Avenue, Frank Spencer Witherbee (3), (Member of Yale's Skull and Bones Society, 1874). John Taylor Johnson (6) built the corner mansion at no. 6 in 1856. His daughter, Frances, inherited the estate upon his death in 1893; she was married to Pierre Mali, Belgium consul-general, and noted for the lavish parties including her daughter's coming-out party splashed in society papers on December 13, 1912. Across 8th Street was the Edison Illumination Company at no. 10. Setting up offices on Fifth Avenue in 1881, Thomas A. Edison's (7) fledging Power Company supplied electricity to fifty-nine customers in a square mile and hotel instruction signage (8). Today, the Edison building remains, but in 1952, that row of mansions was replaced with the twenty-one-floor/353-unit mid-century landmark.

FIFTH & W 10TH: The first house on the left (1) was the first mansion on Fifth Avenue. The Brevoort Mansion at no. 24, built in 1834 with extensive gardens, held its first grand party, inviting the elite of New York to the newly cobbled Fifth Avenue's former dirt road. It was an over-the-top costume affair where among the 600 guests, two eloped—a social scandal eliminating masquerades as an event theme for years. The 10th Street corner mansion at no. 32, according to Dau's *New York Blue Book*, belonged to Amos F. Eno, Jr. (3), son of Amos R. Eno, the owner of the famed Fifth Avenue Hotel (2) at Fifth & 23rd and the Flatiron property (see pages 24–25). *Blue Book* listed Junior as a "Capitalist," but he donated nearly $2 million to the Society of Mechanics & Tradesmen of the City of New York. Further down the street beyond the Episcopal "Church of Ascension" at no. 40 was steamship company magnate and noted sportsman William B. Boulton (4), often set to play at the famed polo grounds further up Fifth Avenue at 110th Street (c. 1876–1889). Below, commanding the entire block between 9th and 10th, the Brevoort mansion with its extensive gardens became the fifteen-story co-op with gardens on the roof in 1926. Mr. Eno's mansion would be razed in 1923 and replaced with a trendy fifteen-story building as would Mr. Boulton's in 1929. The church did not ascend and remains in their shadow.

FIFTH & E 10TH: Mark Twain, Skivvies, and a Murderer: Crossing Fifth, on the far left at no. 39 where a carriage awaits was the starter mansion for William Miller II. A family in U.S. politics, he had just graduated Columbia law school and took possession in 1880, remaining there for thirty-five years with his bride, Edith Warren (1), until they moved uptown to a Beaux-Arts masterpiece. The summer of 1876, at nos. 37 & 35 up to the 10th street corner, the Grosvenor Hotel (2) was built and reluctantly accepted by the neighbors due to its high-clientele and celebs such as Mark Twain (3). Peter F. Collier (4), across 10th and two houses in at no. 29, changed his life from the seminary to publishing to start *Collier's Magazine*. His neighbor, A. J. Scriven (5) at no. 25, made quite another name for himself as the A. Scriven Shirt Co., expanding into the undergarment line, hence deriving being caught dressed only in underwear as "caught in one's 'skivvies.'" Yet the name "Murderer" was attached to Daniel Edgar Sickles (6). Even though while escorting known "lady of the evening," Fanny White, in his travels, he would present her to Queen Victoria while his pregnant wife remained home. Later, in 1859, his jealousy of a reported affair with the D.C. district attorney Philip Key, son of Francis Scott Key (composer of "The Star-Spangled Banner"), seemed to matter. Sickles sent a note on his wife's letterhead as a ploy of a lovers' rendezvous across D.C.'s Lafayette Park where he murdered Key. He pleaded "temporary insanity" (the first use of this defense in U.S. law) and got off. Sickle would later become a general and Civil War hero at Gettysburg, losing a leg.

FIFTH & E 12TH: On the southeast corner at 13th Street stood no. 61, Wernz & Koehne Florists, one of many different florist shops (1) serving the ample needs of Fifth Avenue. On the other northeast corner at 12th Street, no. 53 Fifth, the home of James Lenox (2), the third richest man in New York. He inherited 30 acres between Fourth and Fifth in 1839, where he built his mansion, would buy and keep the Gutenberg Bible, donated land for the church across the street, and live in his manor house until his death in February 1880. The next prominent owner of no. 53 was the "U.S. Aeronautical Reserve" (3). Immediate plans were submitted with media attention to have a landing strip, 250 × 17 feet wide, affixed to their three-story headquarters. Yet with the announcement, in three months, membership rose to 3,200, including President Taft. Earliest enrollees include Wilber and Orville Wright (3), who in 1903 had been credited with man's first flight, choosing who would make the flights with a "flip of a coin." Success would give them new status from bicycle repairmen/builders to Aeronautical Pioneers. Today at no. 53 Fifth Avenue looms a fifteen-story building with no landing strip. Now let us cross the street to visit Mr. Lenox's church.

FIFTH & W 12TH: Known as "Old First," the First Presbyterian Church (1) with Tiffany windows commanded the block between 11th and 12th streets since 1844–46 with the benefaction of James Lenox (2). Just across 12th was the 1847-built home at no. 60 W. Fifth of the prominent Robert Minturn (3). Thursday evenings became the tradition of the all-male millionaires (today billionaires) socials in the Minturn home. During one "social," Robert's wife, Anna, dropped in to suggest they provide a park as a lovely place for the wealthy as well as her four daughters (4) to stroll and ride carriages through while providing a healthy environment for the "poor." Hastening the project was the fact that Robert Minturn owned most of and would donate the land to be become Central Park, fashioned after their visits to Bois de Boulogne and Hyde Park. "Get that landscape designer, Fred Olmsted!" By 1901, nos. 60 and 62 were the homes of the tenth richest man in America, Thomas Ryan (5), seen here in a painting by Joaquin Sorolla. His wealth came from tobacco and public transportation (street cars and subways (IRT)), although against growth of Fifth Avenue, from mansions to monoliths, he gave in and sold in 1915.

FIFTH & W 14TH: Opposition crumbles as do the mansions—the last year of the nineteenth century, 1900, saw the shops and services expanding to retail fashion. Mid-block between 13th and 14th Street was Princess Corsets, foundation garments to "reshape the shape" (1). On the southwest corner was S.W. Steel, featuring the latest fur coats from Paris covering up the reshaping as worn here by the opera singer of the day, Amelita Galli-Curci (2). Across 14th on the northwest corner was the specialty shop of scents of Paris, Pinaud Parfumerie (3). Its founder, Eduard Pinaud (4), started marketing 1830s Europe with fragrances and grooming care products into the twentieth century for both women, featuring their now collectible "vanity cases" a.k.a. "compacts," and men, with the hair and beard-softening shine of Brilliantine (perfume and a colorful oily liquid). His contemporaries in the field were Cody, Chanel, and Christian Dior. In the twenty-first century, the shops and vehicular traffic have changed but the buildings still anchor the intersection.

Fifth & W 15th: From the northwest corner of 14th of the Pinaud Building, no. 90, was Monsieur Pinaud's New York offices of his Paris Perfumes (1), and #92, was H. Seligman Furs. Next was Carlton's Luncheonette for the ladies who lunched and at no. 94, where that single delivery truck waits, was Naething's Restaurant. Just above was perhaps what the truck was waiting for–the Peerless Film Exchange, known for their early movie projectors and lighting equipment; they also handled film promos. The "Exchange" was distributor of early films such as George Méliès' 1902 *A Trip to the Moon* (2). On the corner of 15th were two piano showrooms, Shoningers at no. 96 and, sporting an awning, Wissner's at no. 98 (3). Across 15th was Oppenheimer and Levy, nos. 98–100, for veiling and imported lace to adorn the bride (4). Note the erection of a "sister structure" as seen today, below.

FIFTH & E 14TH: The NE corner of Fifth and 14th extreme left, no. 69, was the Fourteenth St. Suit Store (1), clothing the "Dandies" of the day. Next door, no. 67, was Palm, Fechteler & Co., dealing in transparencies (a.k.a. decals) (2) as the self-described "largest decalcomanie manufacturing company in the world"—décor noted for nineteenth- and twentieth-century home and commercial use from Limoges china to the Louisville Slugger baseball bat. At no. 65 was yet another office of the Edison Co., PR devotee, Edison himself, posing in 1881 on the front steps (3). On the corner at 13th was the Joslyn Filter Co., no. 63, featuring home water filtration systems (4) to purify water through sand and other tank steps to cleanse and calm fears of Yellow Fever and other diseases in drinking water. Upstairs was Hardy & Yerby, tailors (5), keeping Fifth Avenue well dressed. Across 13th, at no. 61, there were flowers to send from what was on page 10, Wernz & Koehne Florists (6). A century later, the entire block was razed to become the location of the 100-year-old The New School, an alternative to the timidity of traditional colleges with a notable staff and alumni from the arts, design, and social sciences.

FIFTH & E 15TH: Laces and safe deposits at 5th and 14th: Just relocated to no. 71 Fifth Avenue from their prosperous enterprise on Broadway is Voss & Stern Laces and Embroidery (est. 1875). Philip Voss sold laces and embroideries and Isaac Stern handle curtains and veilings. Most of their clientele were woman so it was a no-brainer to support the 1909 establishment of "Women's Day" honoring their dedication, hard work, and moral influence in winning World War I. Their PR slogan was "This Woman's Day, Buy War Bond (Brought to you by the 'Laces, Embroideries, Veilings and Ruffling Trade')." Next door was the 14th Street Bank, touting their "safe deposit vaults" (3), where the millionaires of Fifth Avenue could visit their money. Today it is the Chase Bank, established in 1877, and by the 1920s acquiring several smaller banks such as the 14th Street Bank.

FIFTH & W 16TH: Girder framework went up at nos. 98–100, exemplifying residential turning commercial with the norm rising fifteen floors, replacing smaller three- and four-story services shops; land values and innovation in elevators helped. On the other corner of Fifth & W 16th Street, no. 108 was the Union Skirt Co. (1); popular clothes were sold at between $5 and $8, shirtwaists sold separately. For the first ten years of the new century, most skirts would cover down to the ankles and trail along the Fifth Avenue cobbles. The northwest corner, no. 112, was Louis Meyers & Son, glovemakers for the proper dressed men and women of Fifth Avenue. Meyers, as many others, had their sizable "work-rooms" for tanning and assembly out in Gloversville, NY (2), adjacent to Johnstown, soon known as "Glove Cities"—center of the craft. The edifice at no. 112 housed the showroom of E. Jacob & Co. with veils and nettings.

FIFTH & W 18TH: On the southwest corner of 18th Street at no. 126 is Johnson Cowdin Co. with their new stiffer ribbon creating new heights in hat-making (1). The fifteen-story building brought "stereo-graph photography," as seen here on its rooftop (2)—a stereo-card of a photographer perched over the street on 2×4s to catch the right angle. Crossing 18th street was P.K. Wilson & Son Importers at no. 130. Mr. Wilson (3) started the enterprise in 1867, dealing with fine imported fabrics and left a $2 million estate to his son in 1913 ($50 million in today's dollars). Above, crowds out front of no. 134 eye the latest in fine pianos and the Waters Autola, player pianos in Horace Waters & Company (1845–1949, continued by his sons), who handled fine instruments. Mr. Waters (4) (1812–1893) was also known as a frequent collaborator with Stephen Foster, the father of American music. Next door were more fine pianos at 140 Fifth Avenue with Hardman, Peck, & Co. (est. 1842)—makers of the official piano of the New York Metropolitan Opera Company.

FIFTH & E 18TH: The "Lace Hankie Code": On the east side of Fifth at 18th at no. 95 was Julius Strauss & Co., where perchance our model, in full lace (1), would have found the perfect ladylike way to attract a gentleman's attention—a perfumed lace hankie. Next door, at nos. 87–89 was to be Marshal Field's (2) as a New York location, but this never came to fruition; Field's death in New York in 1906 perhaps altered the company's plans. At no. 85 was Houghton Mifflin Co. (3), one of the largest education publishers of standardized tests and textbooks in 1916, but infamously in 1961, they passed on printing, Julia Child's *Mastering the Art of French Cooking*. Across 17th at no. 79 was Stern & Stern, chiffon importers (4), adding to milady's choices in fabrics. Surely, actress Geraldine Farrar (5), as well as this jogger below, knew the pros of a wave of an arm.

FIFTH & E 19TH: More fabrics on Fifth with Lord and Taylor, which was originally established in lower Manhattan in 1826 but moved uptown, developing two sites—one in 1906 at nos. 111 & 113, Fifth & 19th (1), now a Victoria's Secret, the other at Fifth & 39th by 1909. The corner of 18th was Goldenberg Bros. & Co., no. 109, the largest dealer in fine lace. The next generation growing up in the business, Samuel Goldenberg, in 1904, penned *Lace: Its Origin and History* (2). He and his wife were survivors of the *Titanic*, wearing only their woolen pajamas, perhaps from S. Stein and Co. Woolens (3), neighbors at no. 107. Next door was Bamberg & Risser Silks, on the ground floor of no. 103, and upstairs was former woolen dealers, now silks from their looms (4) of A.H. Rice. Cohen Bros. & Co., at no. 99 Fifth, specialized in machined lace curtains (5), targeting 1910 home décor.

Fifth & W 20th: The southwest corner at no. 152 was F. Schumacher and Co. (est. 1889), creators of the upholstery and wall coverings of Fredrick Schumacher (1), founder, providing the best in decor for the White House, the Capitol, and grand Fifth Avenue manors as well as films and TV like *Gone with the Wind*, *My Fair Lady*, *Gigi*, *The Age of Innocence*, and even *I Love Lucy*. Across 20th was Geo. P. Ide & Co. (est. 1865) for shirts and collars (2), and on the ground floor at no. 154 was the trunk and luggage firm of Crouch and Fitzgerald (3) (est. 1839), coveted today as then, fulfilling a tourist's need for steamer trunks for the "Grand Tour." Mid-block, no. 158 was the Fleming H. Revell Publishers (4), dealing as a Christian press for more than 145 years, with *Robert's Rules of Order* among its publications. The Mohawk Building (*c*. 1893, no. 160) was built by E.H. Ingen & Co., who occupied most of it while dealing with fine woolens; trade lore has it that Edward Hook Van Ingen, whose home was further up Fifth, made no fewer than 178 Atlantic crossings—a remarkable task in the nineteenth century—to secure imported cloth weave standards for his refined customers.

FIFTH & W 22ND: E. F. Foley photographer, at 164 Fifth Avenue, specialized in studio photography not just for the wealthy but public relations for Broadway actors as John McCormack and Mme Luisa Tetrazzini, c. 1909 (1); after all, this was the theatre district. At no. 168 was renowned educator and superintendent of NYC public schools William H. Maxwell (2). Crossing 22nd, the corner at no. 172 was one of many Western Union telegraph cable offices (3) throughout Manhattan; above was brokerage firm of Sternberger, Sinn & Co. (4). Third floor was the milliner workroom of A. D. Burgesser & Co. for women's "be-feathered hats," befitting of an Easter Parade down Fifth Avenue, but they also sold to dealers across America and Canada. Past no. 174, the awning of Mirror Candies was Dunlap & Co. (5), no. 178, famed for their collapsible top hats, plus the 4-inch-tall hatbox for easy packing. Robert Dunlap, age twelve in 1857, had been an errand boy for Charles Knox of Knox Hats, working his way up with little requested compensation, hence striking out on his own to success.

FIFTH & E 21ST: Schribner's & Sons, NY, besides launching paperbacks, has the distinction of having their "printer's mark" (1) painted in the north corridor ceiling arch in the Library of Congress, Washington, D.C. Above and center, another arch was the entry to Bonwits, Harris & Co. at no. 151. In the 1880s, Paul Bonwit's start-up was a small millinery shop with several partners, one being Mr. Harris; growth would be destined in 1898 with Edmund D. Teller as "Bonwit Teller." Their pronouncement was: "An uncommon display of wearing apparel from foreign and domestic sources at moderate prices." At the time, a "proper" woman out alone was taboo, so a department store catering to women (2) would change the culture, as did Bonwits, when in the 1930s they hired a woman, Hortense Odlum, as president of Bonwits, the first of a major U.S. department store. Across 21st at no. 141, the ornate oval window was one of eight Manhattan locations of Park & Tilford, a chain of fancy groceries. Joseph Park and John Tilford were ambitious fellow clerks; as friends, they struck out in 1840 to cater to the wealth of Fifth Avenue with their own brand names (3), sounding like the sequel to the final scene of *Hello Dolly*.

FIFTH & E 22ND: It is the least photographed side of the "Flatiron" at 22nd Street. Years prior in 1884 (1), a collection of shops and brownstones, the tallest being developer Amos Eno's seven-story apartment building with a perfect north-facing wall for "pickle promo-signage." One of the earliest tenants of the new Flatiron building at no. 167 was S.M. Brittingham & Co., haberdashers in a day when a hat came with a "hatbox" (2). Across to the SE 22nd corner at no. 159, on the second floor were the executive offices of O.J. Gude, innovator of outdoor advertising, including the space on Amos Eno's building. Gude, with a startup capital of $100, was the first to do electric lighting with the Heinz "glowing pickle" (3) bathing the neighborhood in pickle-green at a time when most surrounding apartments had no electricity. At street level, no. 157, was Abm. Besthoff & Son, fine leather goods, and next door at 157A were the three Pach Brothers Photographers (est. 1860s), servicing the elite and theatrical (4). World-renowned publisher Charles Scribner's Sons (5) on the far right, with the striking remaining edifice, would set the presses at no. 155 Fifth.

FIFTH & 23RD AND BROADWAY INTERSECTION: a photographer (below, *c.* 1900) plies his trade recording one of several "arches" just before the block behind him, including the "pickle," made way for the iconic "Fuller Building" in 1902; it was famously known as the "Flatiron," a name attributed to the triangle lot long before construction. Among the tallest at the time, its height created an updraft that would blow women's skirts and elicit wolf whistles; this prompted constables on patrol, at Fifth and 23rd, to skidoo them away, hence the expression: "23 Skidoo." Today, a well-photographed twenty-two-story building, especially at this angle, only appearing as the skinniest structure in the world.

FIFTH & W 23RD: Erected between the front of the Amos R. Eno-owned first Fifth Avenue Hotel and across from Madison Square Park was the original George Washington Inauguration Commemorative Arch, *c.* 1889 (1), but would be replaced a few years later with the Admiral George Dewey Victory Arch (1899–1901) (2), probably the one being photographed on p. 24. Two other arches would be erected, one at 26th and the last of the victory arches (3), at 24th that honors the city's dead in the Great War, later to be known as World War I.

FIFTH & W 24TH ST: On the west side in 1852 was a stagecoach stop, Madison Cottage (a.k.a. "Corporal Thompson's Roadhouse") (1), but by 1853, it was cleared to make way for Franconi's Hippodrome (2) under a big top of canvas and wood to accommodate 10,000 to watch "amusements of ancient Greeks and Romans." After two years of glee, developer, Amos Eno built the "Fifth Avenue Hotel," no. 200 (3), complete with Otis Tufts' five-floor elevator, an innovation that lured guests the likes of Buffalo Bill Cody (4) to Pres. Ulysses S. Grant. The Fifth Avenue Building, later as the "Toy Center," replaced the hotel by 1909. Just across 24th Street with a Broadway address was the Albemarle Hotel, built of white marble next to the "Hoffman House" (5)—for men only. Far right, the Berlitz language school was founded in 1878 by Maximilian Berlitz (6), mastering languages and that corner at 202 W Fifth with its six-story brick building since 1886.

THROUGH TIME IN MADISON SQUARE: Above is an image of Madison Square Park in 1908, but prior, between 1882 and 1886, the square was perfect then for the happening of the "Theatre District," the home of the torch segment of the Statue of Liberty (1). It was a temporary attraction to raise funds for the base soon to be set in the harbor; a contribution of 50 cents allowed one to ascend the arm. Since 1916, only workers ascend to inspect, repair, or maybe change a light bulb, save for actor Norman Lloyd in Hitchcock's 1942 film *Saboteur*, who fell cinematically to his dramatic death. The convention hall, seen rising center, was Madison Square Garden (2), one of several incarnations built by the Vanderbilt family between 1879 and 1926. The topped-out sculpture, *Diana* (3), was whispered to have been modeled on one of designer Stanford White's young lady friends, resulting in White's murder by her crazed jealous husband not dealing well with those whispers of her teenage peccadillos. "The Garden" became home to political conventions and trade shows (4). Far right, between two large buildings, the "Met Life Tower" goes up thirty floors (5) between 1908 and 1910, modeled, except for the clocks, after the Campanile in Venice, Italy. All four clocks were set to the right time on opening day.

FIFTH & 26TH: Further up Fifth Avenue is yet another arch erected along Madison Square Park. Presented on April 30 1889, it was honoring the centennial of George Washington's first presidential election, but was planned to be a little less permanent than the one in Washington Square. The image also illustrates the number of trendy bowler hats as far as the eye will allow and catches the power of an avenue parade as they pass the old Brunswick Hotel, which by 1906 would be replaced as below.

FIFTH & E 27TH: The Brunswick Building, no. 225 Fifth replaced, in 1906, the old Brunswick Hotel and a collection of shops, including the no. 229 location of the Detroit Photo Co. (1), recorder of late 1800s New York imagery. Since 2004, it has been revered as the "Grand Madison," but when built, it was labeled as a "vulgar brick horror" by architectural critics. Incarnations included a hotel, several showrooms, offices (in 1955, the offices of "Tupperware"), and at one time street frontage for Brentano's Books (2), which had been established in 1853 as a newsstand in front of the New York Hotel. Next door at was the Raymond-Whitcomb & Co. (3), commercial travel agents with Metropolitan Museum of Art and the Smithsonian as clientele; later, in 1999, it was entangled in a $400,000 U.S. postage dispute. On the other side of the building's vaulted entrance was another location of Park & Tilford's fancy groceries and candies (4), eventually a site bought by Woolworth's in 1929; yes a five-&-dime on Fifth. Above Park & Tilford were the real estate developer's offices of Long Beach Estates (5), launching Long Beach, NY, a resort, now a bedroom community and childhood home of Billy Crystal.

FIFTH & W 26TH: Below, beyond the awning of the Brunswick Building, are the changes across Fifth. Above, at no. 202 was the Berlitz School; at no. 206 was Theo B. Starr, silversmith; and no. 208 was Lincoln Trust Co. Next door was Mark Cross, selling harness and leather goods. Founded 1845 in Boston by Henry W. Cross, he named his store for his young son, Mark. This branch at no. 210, seen with a horse drawn coach trotting by (1), opened in 1902 dealing with Manhattan's need for fine saddles; today, it stocks fine handbags. On the corner at no. 212, the place to be seen was Delmonico's, serving the best steak in New York (1876–1902), before moving up to Fifth and 44th. Taking over the lease, brothers Jean and Louis Martin refurbished it in the latest *art-nouveau* style (2) and opened as Café Martin in 1902. The menu (3) from February 10, 1910, was touting staying open all night, obliging guests from the Metro-Ball at Madison Square Garden with a *prix fixe* menu, $1.50 to 2—noticing among the extras: ½ dozen oysters, 60 cents. The grand entrance was on 26th facing the six-story Victoriana (4), home of Meriden Silver Co., on street level, razed in 1911 for the present high-rise, center.

FIFTH & W 27TH: At no. 224 Fifth Avenue was Frank Brothers (1), haberdashers and designers of men's and women's superior footwear since 1865. A couple of shops north at no. 228 was celebrity photographer Charles L. Ritzmann, whose collection of images of the famous, mid-1800s, and Gilded Age, by 1882, would dub this gallery as the "Palace of Photographic Celebrity" (2), brokering images for fans and magazines into the twentieth century. Next door was the hosiery business (est. 1888) of brothers Peck and Peck (3). Rumor has it that they had to pay a distrusting landlord their rent once every twenty-four hours. Eventually with other more congenial landlords, they would have seventy-eight stores across the country. Crossing W. 7th Street were several haberdashers (4)—Charles T. Jones at no. 232; Josephson Bros. at no. 234; and Smith and Gary Clothiers at no. 238. Edward Smith had started out in 1833 as a cutter/tailor/fitter, who realized the only clothing available for boys was "made to measure" so he pioneered "ready-mades" for children (5), becoming the leader in that industry. The largest retail space on the block at no. 240 was the luxurious Frette linens of the day with the Fifth Avenue Linen Store.

FIFTH & W 28TH: Now emerging as Smith, Gary and Co., beside boy's ready-made clothes, they would also become known as the supplier of New York police uniforms (1). More tailor operations were in the upper floors at nos. 242, 244, and 246, but street level at no. 242 (which had been the Republican headquarters since 1887) became Dobbs & Co. (est. 1908), best known for their gent's silk hats, opera hats, canes, umbrellas, and their visually famous hat boxes (2). Across 28th at no. 254 was Yamanaka & Co. (covering all five floors), with Yamanaka Sadajir, 山中定次郎, (3), the renowned expert on Japanese and Chinese art. As it was the Theatre District, here were the actor's photo studios of Napoleon Sarony, no. 256, (4, self-portrait) and upstairs, the studios of Braun, Clement & Co.; the latter was also noted as nineteenth- and twentieth-century heliographers (5). Theodore Marceau (6) had his theatrical photo studio at no. 258 with clients such as Sarah Bernhardt, Andrew Carnegie, and one of George Méliès' film stars, Mlle Lottie (*c.* 1899, 7). Marceau also achieved financial success by buying real estate on the avenue. Today, in a web of scaffold, Fifth Avenue continues.

FIFTH & W 31ST.: Gilman Collamore & Co. (est. 1861) was a multi-generation company of fine porcelain, rivaling Tiffany and Co. and Black Starr & Frost. By 1890, they occupied the first two floors of the Wilbraham Building, at no. 284 (1), with the upper floors exclusively bachelor flats. Next door, now a vacant lot in waiting, no. 292, was the fine fabric trends of Mme. Najla Mogabgab (2). One floor up was the photo studio to the affluent The Misses Selby, sisters Emily and Lillian. Emily would photograph one of the last images of the Lindberg Baby (3). At no. 294 was the importer and maker of fashionable furs of George Booss (4) (est. 1853) "for seasonal fur storage, telephone 159 Madison." On the corner of 31st, at no. 298, was the Mauser Mfg. Co., silversmiths (5) and at no. 302, Henry Duveen (6) established his gallery in the 1870s, dealing with Rembrandts and Italian renaissance masterpieces. He also owned some of the rarities of philately, including the "Miss Rose" cover franked with a pair of British Guiana "cotton reels" and the very rare Hawaiian Missionary 2c and 13c stamps (7). Upon his death in 1919, his collection proceeds—then over $680,000—were given to the Royal Ear Hospital in London.

On the southeast corner, at no. 243, was the mansion of William Duncan, who had sold out in 1872 to the Knickerbocker Club, a contrary group of old and *nouveau riche*, former Union Club members, which ten years later would sell to developers, who retained the name for the Knickerbocker Apts. (1). In 1925, it would make way for the twenty-four-story office building. Next door, at no. 241, was the Florida East Coast Co. (est. 1892) by Standard Oil's 25 percent partner Henry Flagler (2), promoting Florida as a vacation spot for New Yorkers, thus beginning the tradition of the summer retreat. On the same block at no. 237 was the New York location of E. B. Meyrowitz, a pioneer in the optical community since 1875. Aside for his fine eyewear popular with presidents ("Teddy to Ike"), his "goggles for early air and auto travel were a must" (3). At no. 235 was the branch of Martin & Martin (4), harness and saddlery to the queen. Fine jewelry could be found at Pickslay & Co. (5) at no. 233, and upstairs was Birdsey, Somers and Co., creating "the handsome form" as ladies undergarments; ironically today at that northeast corner is the Museum of Sex.

FIFTH & E 29TH: On the northeast corner was the social Calumet Club (est. 1879), which had moved to this four-story mansion (no. 267) in 1887. The name "Calumet" related to the Indian peace pipe; club secretary, H. O. Tallmadge (1), gave a dinner on December 22, 1894, inviting five prominent golf course clubs to form the "Amateur Golf Association of the United States," soon to be dropping the amateur for today's "USGA"; the executive committee is seen above in 1897 (2). The Woman's Tournament Committee was formed in 1917; Kate C. Hartley (3) swings a "winner." The other corner at no. 263 was the Pennsylvania Railroad Co., and at no. 261 was A. L. Audrain and Co., wholesale and fancy goods dealer. Most of the street-level shops, like A. J. Crawford Co. Antiques at no. 255 and C. V. Miller at no. 257, specializing in Louis the XIV antiques (4), offered fine period decor. Above the shops were tailor fitting and tailors' workrooms (5): Alfred Nelson Co. at no. 261, and at no. 259, Stone Suits, Loughrey & Son, A. de Salvo, and E. B. Ellison Co. woolens. Today, do not look for that four-story Calumet Club mansion (6); it has gone, leaving its neighbor at no. 267 remaining. The corner was replaced in 1912 with an eleven-floor building.

35

FIFTH & E 31ST: A few shops from the corner were Dunne & Co. tailors at no. 297, next to the high quality of the Behning Piano Co. At no. 295, the noted expert on jade and his stock of Chinese curios was Long Sang Ti, writer of *Chinese Jade: Why Called "Lucky Stone"* (1). In 1900, making quite a name as a fifteen-year-old entrepreneur was Mary Elizabeth (2) and her "Mary Elizabeth Tearoom" at no. 291. Her fame and public relations derived from her candies and that, by 1913, she signed a million-dollar twenty-one-year lease with an all-woman business operation. Her tearoom at street level would also exhibit a few photographs of New York, luring interested parties to the attic gallery, at no. 291 (3), of Arthur Stieglitz (4), well-known photo-artist and husband to artist Georgia O'Keeffe (5), premiering her *Southwest* and *Skyscraper* work. He also introduced the Fifth Avenue art investors to new European artists, including Pablo Picasso. Further north at no. 287 was the London & Northwest Rails New York office, promoting their Postal Mail Line steamships. Beyond at no. 285 were the oil paintings of the J. H. Strauss gallery. Crossing 30th on the SE corner was the International Sleeping Car Co., founded by George Nagelmackers (6), who had been impressed by his youthful travels across 1867 America on Pullman night trains. Adopting the same, he catered to wealthy travelers across Europe and Asia, including the famed *Orient Express*. By 1894, the Compagnie International des Grands Hotel was founded as a subsidiary and began operating a chain of luxury hotels in major cities, becoming the inspiration of the film, *Grand Hotel*; the closing line came from Lionel Barrymore, when questioned if there is a "Grand Hotel" in Paris: "There's a Grand Hotel everywhere in the world!"

FIFTH & E. 32ND: George. H. Everall, noted sport-wear designer, lived at no. 327; he was the Calvin Klein of his day: each metal button and waist-label bore the moniker, "Geo. H. Everall/New York." Antiques of Baumgarten & Co. were at no. 323, while the white building above at no. 321 was Theodore A. Kohn and Sons, recognized for their jewelry, their expertise of precious stones, and Theo's writings on the subject (1). Also available were tins of "boxwood" sawdust to assist in dry cleaning of pocket watches. The northeast corner at no. 319 became a new location of the Knickerbocker Club, retaining their very exclusive British and Dutch aristocratic family lineage; their entrance from 32nd Street was meant to show that exclusivity (2). The next block was Sohmer & Co. at no. 315, with Mason & Hamlin, piano showrooms, were no. 313. Every fine home on Fifth Avenue had to have a piano, and every refined young lady had to be able to play (3). Two matching row-mansions (nos. 311 & 309) belonged to Carola, the countess de Laugier-Villars, and her sister, Estella Livingston Redmond. Very philanthropic with family money, Carola did what so many of New York socialites hoped their daughters would do; she married a titled man in 1893. At no. 303 was Schwarz Toy Bazaar, launched in New York in 1870 from Baltimore; Fredrick August Otto Schwarz soon renamed it "F. A. O. Schwarz," a visual treat for any young at heart the minute they walked in (4).

FIFTH & W 32ND: On the southwest corner at no. 318 was the Kaskel and Kaskel Building (1), a historic structure, c. 1902, built for their haberdashery but after unsuccessful attempts to preserve the building, it was torn down in 2017 for a planned slender forty-story building. The smaller image, left, below matched up in time warp panorama, was taken just days before it was demolished. The next block, no. 320, was the silversmith Reed and Barton (2) (1824–2015); now its ornate entrance is obliterated in CVS style. Dwight R. MacAfee Antiques, above at no. 324, seems to be showing off its large reduction sale banner. The fine gems of William Reiman, no. 328, are primo-collectable today via Heritage Auction House (4). Walk Over Shoes, no. 330, was the New York location of the 250-year-old international firm. In "High-button" shoes days, instead of a shoehorn, a buttonhook tool (5) was given with each pair sold. One of the largest chain stores in America, the United Cigar Co. (est. 1901), at no. 334, eventually handled the famed Mickey Mouse watch. Last on the block was the Jamaica Estates Real Estates offices promoting 2-acre lots among rolling hills of an early 1900s planned restricted all-white community largely impenetrable to minorities, in the middle of Queens; reportedly, Fred Trump's choice for his family as an oasis from the diversity of the rest of that borough.

1 2 3 4 5 6

FIFTH & W 34TH: The Astor acres (5 acres per block): gifted in 1854 by patriarch William Backhouse Astor to his sons to build mansions for the next generation, this fueled feuds by subsequent spouses. With a garden and a large fountain between the houses, each threatened to raze their houses to build smelly stables. Instead in 1893, William Waldorf Astor, then the richest man in America, replaced his residence at no. 338 with the thirteen-floor Waldorf Hotel, dominating the block and the home of his aunt, Caroline Schermerhorn Astor (3), at no. 350 Fifth. She was known to snub the Vanderbilts as they were from new money (by her own declaration). She had built a grand ballroom (4) at the back of the home to accommodate the cream of New York society, establishing them and the term, for the *sacred* "Four Hundred." After building the Waldorf, she tired of being gawked at by tourists, so her son, John Jacob Astor IV (5), persuaded her to move up Fifth Avenue in 1897, and he built an even larger sixteen-floor hotel, the Astoria, connected by what was called Peacock Alley and soon became the Waldorf-Astoria (6), with an entrance from the 34th Street side. John Jacob Astor IV would go down with the *Titanic*; William Waldorf Astor would take his millions to England, and the hotel would be replaced in 1929–1930 with 109 floors of the Empire State Building at 350 Fifth Avenue.

FIFTH & W 35TH: Originally founded in 1879 as Lilliputian Bazaar, Albert Best moved to no. 372 Fifth as Best & Co. in 1908. His children's clothing specialized in gender-identified garments, getting little boys out of the gowns as formal wear and into pants—a trend that had gone unchanged since the sixteenth century. At no. 384 was famed furrier A. Jaeckel (1) and on the other corner was the Gorman Co. Silversmiths, supplying tea service to the White House as well as the America's Cup for yachting, and the Davis Cup for tennis. In 1818, Jabez Gorham (2) had begun in a one-room shop as a precious metal jeweler. By 1841, well-established, his son, John Gorman (3), joined the firm, and Gorham Manufacturing Company was destined to be a giant in the world of silver extending into the twenty-first century. The northwest corner, at no. 392, was the home of successful stockbroker Louis T. Holt. Next door, at no. 394, was De Pinna Importers (4) (est. 1885), providing tailored suits for women, such as Vesta Tilley, as seen in their ads. At no. 396 was an American inventor, actor, and entrepreneur, Isaac Merritt Singer (5), with his Singer Sewing Machine Co. Aside his prolificacy in patents, Singer fathered at least twenty-four children with various wives and mistresses, mostly in and out of the families of Fifth Avenue, maintaining multiple homes on the avenue for them. He was arrested for bigamy but fled to London. Next door at no. 398 was Tecla Jewelers (6) of Paris, London, and New York.

FIFTH & W 37TH: At no. 400 was the Landay Brothers, featuring the innovations of the Victor Talking Machine Co. Artist Francis Barraud's family dog was "'Nipper', listening to his master's voice" (1), who became the company symbol in 1900 and would be acquired in 1929, throughout different mergers, by RCA. At the corner at no. 404 was Davis Collamore & Co., importer of fine porcelain and glass headed up by Davis Collamore (1820–1887) (2), carrying on a family tradition along with his brother, Gilman Collamore, whose shop was at Fifth and W 31st. Across W 37th at no. 412 was the Brick Presbyterian Church, originally established in 1767, this its second location 1858 to 1940 as seen from E 37th (3) until wishes of the congregation to move further uptown to Park Avenue and 91st. For Mrs. Caroline Schermerhorn Astor Wilson (4), the daughter of William Backhouse Astor, the mansion at no. 414 Fifth and 38th (5) had been a wedding gift from her father in 1884, even though the family disapproved of her future in-laws. She eventually sold it to Franklin Simon in 1903 for his flagship department store, with forty-two locations across the country bearing his name, specializing in woman's fashions and furnishings (6) until closing in 1977.

FIFTH & E 34TH ST.: Benjamin Altman, born in Manhattan in 1840, went into the dry goods business by age twenty-five, rapidly establishing B. Altman & Co. at no. 357 Fifth as his flagship store (1906–1989). The atrium interior, seen *c.* 1909 (1), beckoned customers to explore the store's floors. Wrapped around by B. Altmans, architecturally, at no. 355, was M. Knoedler & Co., art dealership (est. 1846; interior seen here 2). Initially filling the many walls of mansions on Fifth with art, it would close in 2011, supposedly amid lawsuits for fraud, ending 165 years as the oldest commercial gallery. Below, with the corner Knoedler's building gone and filled in seamlessly with the addition to the former B. Altman's, it is now the City University of NY's Graduate Center. Across 34th Street was the no. 353 building accommodating W.W. Harrison Co., a walking stick firm supplying all the "swells" the prestige of strolling down the avenue, such as the earl of Minto (3). Noting when the upper panorama was taken, January 21, 1910, the ground floor was the showroom of Chester Billings & Son, jewelry/silversmiths in a prime location (rent: $45,000 a year). The paper signage "Public Auction" (4) showed the seventy-year-old firm was now bankrupt, a victim of the panic of October of 1907. The rest of the frontage was Fox, Stiefel & Co., motoring apparel offering "dusters and goggles" (5), when "parading" in open cars on the avenue.

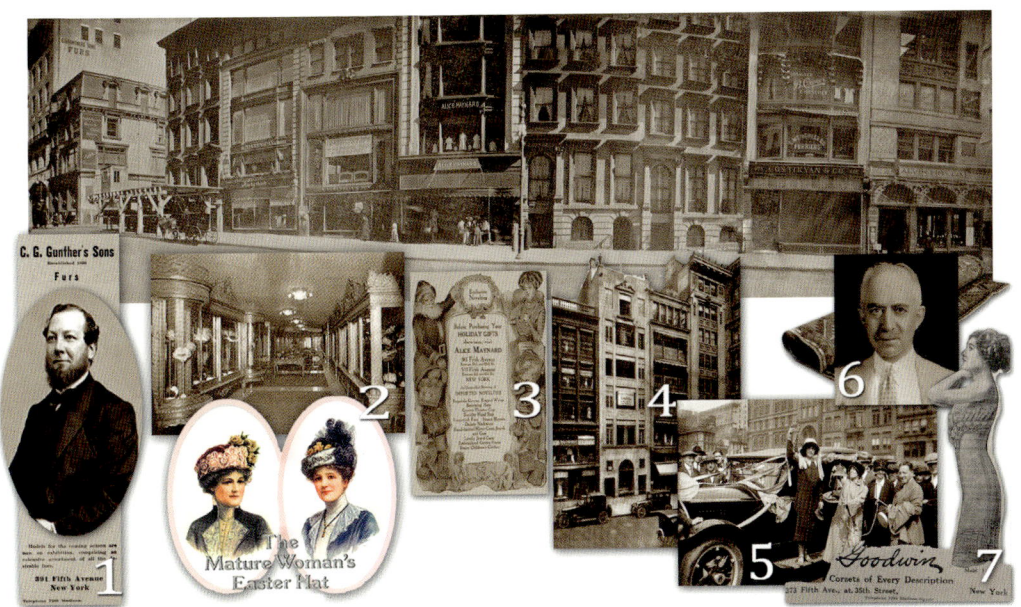

FIFTH & E 36TH: Adjoining the Tiffany Building in 1909 was the Gunther Building, nos. 391–3 with the showroom for C. G. Gunther's Sons, Furrier (est. 1820) by Gunther, Sr. His son, Charles G. Gunther (1), would be mayor of New York (1864–1866) before entering the family business. One of the top milliners represented in the annual Easter Parade was Charles C. Kurzman (2) and his plush showcases displaying his hats at no. 385. Next door, A. Lowenbein's Furniture, at no. 383, would be razed along with no. 381, Alice Maynard, ladies' wear" (3) in 1920 replaced by six stories still there today. Socialite and one of Mrs. Astor's "the Four Hundred" was John Hadden, who bought the former home at no. 379 of Commodore Cornelius Vanderbilt, the patriarch of the Vanderbilt family. No. 377 was the home of Gordon Norrie, but it too would be remodeled in 1919—brownstone to limestone façade (4)—as "Child's Restaurant" with upper shops. The widow Norrie (5), waving farewell, retreated to her country home. No. 375 was S. Kent Costikyan (6), dealer in fine carpets, while upstairs, no. 373 was Goodwin Corsets (7), reshaping the bustled women.

FIFTH & E 37TH: Above at no. 415, the lone building on the E. 38th /37th block was the gallery of William Schaus, fine art dealer, handling artist John Gast's *Maud Muller Leaning on Her Rake* (1868) (1), destined for a Fifth Avenue client, as were the vacant lots also destined for development. At the SE corner of 37th was Louis Comfort Tiffany (2), who had already made a name for his art and glass creations of Art Nouveau, including the full wall of stained glass in the White House when, as design director, he joined his late father, Charles Louis Tiffany's thriving jewelry business, Tiffany & Co. (est. 1837), moving to their fourth location (3), no. 393, in 1902. The famous 9-foot figure of Atlas holding a 4-foot clock (4) by Henry Fredrick Metzler was commissioned by Tiffany, Sr., back in 1853 and has graced the entrance of every Tiffany location since; it currently resides at no. 727 Fifth Avenue, appearing in the opening of *Breakfast at Tiffany's*.

FIFTH & E 39TH: The large Victorian building on the northeast corner (1881–1932 when destroyed by fire) was the Union League, a political movement evolving into a social organization and a supporter of the United States Sanitary Commission, a forerunner of the Red Cross. The six founders, pictured (2), include Frederick Law Olmsted, designer of Central Park. The block beyond had two prestigious piano companies—the piano delivery wagon is in front of Knabe Piano Co., no. 437, now a Payless, and Hardman Piano, no. 433, seen in re-construction. Between them at no. 435 was the British Benson & Hedges, tobacconist. Richard Benson, a heavy cigar smoker, died of lung cancer in 1885, the same year his partner, William Hedges, had died and was succeeded by his son, Alfred (3). John M. Crapo was next door, no. 431, with fine Italian linens, showed off his store with an image on the cover of his catalog (4). Henry Augustus Siebrecht Florists, no. 427, had an amply winter supplies of orchards direct from his greenhouses, while no. 425, the Siebrecht Building (5), was for his other ventures. Famed as a top horticulturist, he introduced the striking, albeit smelly, yellow Japanese and Chinese ginkgo trees into autumn popularity.

FIFTH & W 39TH: From the corner of 38th Street was Joseph P. Hennessy, no. 424, Bronx Department of Parks and investigator of Tammany Hall corruption in 1913. G.C. Thibault Clean & Dyeing at no. 426 was next to John Fenning Arts & Antiques (1), at no. 428 (est. 1889). Noted auctioneer of many of the disappearing mansions, Fennings held its final auction on March 20, 1913, and soon, Lord & Taylor's eleven-story flagship store would level most of the block, including M. J. Whaley, Stationers (no. 430), Maison Benoit, lingerie (no. 430), J. I. Phipps and Co. (no. 432), Green's Imported Gowns (no. 434), and the hats of Rose Hagan (upstairs). Black, Starr & Frost jewels would remain. The firm, founded by Isaac Marquand (2), dating back to 1810, with several member and name changes, would move in 1898 to no. 438. It coined the term "carriage trade" (see carriage above), referring to their elite clientele that would arrive thus. They also had installed the first plate-glass for window-shopping on the avenue. In 1953, Marilyn Monroe (3) would sing their praises in "♪Diamonds are a Girl's Best Friend.♪" Across 39th Street is the strangest mansion on Fifth, the Wendel Estate, at no. 442. Seven sisters, controlled by a father and brother, rarely socialized, had no phone or electricity, and withered together behind its walls. The last survivor, Ella, was seen counting the days (4), leaving it all in 1931 to her poodle, Toby, who went "developer-dog," soon had the house (5) razed and the dog's relieving yard became a high-rise.

FIFTH & W 40TH: Olga Petrova (1), vaudeville and silent film star, in her riding hat, representing Knox Hatter, at no. 452, which had relocated to the converted Lawrence Kipp Mansion in 1899, just across from the soon to be closing Croton Reservoir, seen here in 1865 (2). The reservoir had served Manhattan's water needs since 1843 with a rooftop promenade for Sunday strolls. In May 1902, the cornerstone was laid for the New York Public Library. It was expected to take three years, while the two stone lions waited to flank the entrance in storage (3); it opened in 1911. President Taft and 50,000 people were in attendance; the final cost was $9 million. Today, visitors can still see a bit of the reservoir foundation in the south-side stairwell. The pair of lions, out of storage, welcome all to its collection—more than 1 million volumes, marking a real reservoir of knowledge.

FIFTH & E 41ST: The block that faces the library was made up of interior design and furniture store in 1910 while just thirty years before, looking south, all homes (1) faced the city reservoir. Irene Hayes (2) had talked her way into opening Irene Hayes Wadley & Smythe Florists thanks to being a "Ziegfeld Girl." This business was thriving, accommodating Fifth Avenue's tremendous fashionable floral needs. Robert Graves Co. at no. 485, showroom and catalog (3), featuring fine wall coverings, was next to Peck & Peck, featuring fine hosiery while on the corner was Frederic's Pearl Shop, no. 479; note the window shoppers peering at the fine pearls. On the southeast corner at no. 477 was H. Van Slochen, dealer of Old Masters art, also filling fashionable home needs, while Farmer's Loan & Trust Co. at no. 475 financed the mansions. For milady, Ufland Millinery Co. at no. 471 would create feathered masterpieces.

FIFTH & E 44TH TO 43RD: Delmonico's (1) at the northeast corner has moved numerous times from William Street in 1827 through more than one Fifth Avenue location as one of the top prestige restaurants in New York. This location, no. 531 (1897–1923), with several banquet rooms (2), accommodated famous patrons such as "Diamond Jim" Brady and Lillian Russell, usually entertaining guests Charles Dickens, Oscar Wilde, J. P. Morgan, and Mark Twain. Prohibition in 1923 ended the original family involvement, selling off the only asset—the famous name. The Harriman National was on the other corner at no. 527. At no. 523 was the Fifth Avenue location of The Hayden Company, quality European antique reproductions. Pictured (3) are their craftsmen in their Rochester, NY, workroom. Upstairs was Kehoe Furs for both men and women, offering raccoon coats for the new open-air motorcars. In 1868, Temple Emanu-El erected a Moorish Revival structure (4) on the northeast corner of 43rd, which was eventually demolished in 1927 for commercial development.

FIFTH & E 45TH: The staff of Lewando's, French dry cleaners (1), pose out front of no. 555, one of several locations. Specializing in handling whalebone garments as well as exchanging bone for metal stays, they also focused on cleaning men and women's white gloves—a continual fashion requirement. Page & Shaw, serving sweets nationwide (1888–1960), was next door at no. 553. The Church of the Heavenly Rest (2) at no. 551 (1868–1924), also opened a soup kitchen to feed the poorest New Yorkers a block away from Delmonico's, which was serving the wealthiest New Yorkers. John N. Golding (3), real estate broker, made millions handling the mansion sales from his office at no. 547. The Lorraine at no. 545 was built in 1898; it rose fourteen floors from street level. At no. 543 was Margaret Murtha, ladieswear, including the latest in 1910 gowns, the pantaloon (4). Another Victor Radio Sales outlet was next door, at no. 541. The end of the block was the famed Delmonico's restaurant, allowing ladies dining alone since 1868 (5). Below today, two images show north and south of Fifth and E 45th.

FIFTH & E 47TH TO 46TH: When Jay Gould (1) died in 1892, he left his four children between $65 and $70 million and the Gould mansion (2) on the northeast corner of Fifth. Helen, his daughter, would remain while her siblings moved on. Although described in 1913 at her wedding at age forty-five (3) as "plain, plump and not much concerned with 'Society'," she was adept at charity work, turning the Gould family robber baron name to philanthropic while becoming the "best loved woman in the country." Across E 47th, the Windsor Arcade had replaced the Windsor Hotel (4), which had been built in 1872 but lost to a horrific fire on St. Patrick's Day 1899. In the parade hoopla, watchers were slow to notice the columns of smoke coming out of the hotel. Rooftop screams were not heard at first until they leapt into the crowds below, drawing attention to others appearing at the windows quickly consumed by the flames, as were all seven floors. Replaced in 1901, the Arcade would become the pioneering temple of refined commerce—a forerunner of the shopping mall; a three-story Beaux-Arts prize of the Gilded Age, its ornate center arch receiving hansom cab to its courtyard shops and offices, one being Worthington Whitehouse's (5). As one of Mrs. Astor's sacred society, the Four Hundred, a confirmed bachelor, he was a well-known "walker," taking her to ballroom socials of some of the wealthiest women of Fifth Avenue, contacts that increased his family fortunes via real estate offices at no. 537. "Walkers" (a.k.a. escorts) just as today, were often gay men sociably suitable for single lady chaperones. Above the arch was the art gallery of collector Henry Reinhardt (6), patron to the National Gallery. Besides shopping for a Steinway piano, one could have their kerosene lamps rewired at Dardonvilles at no. 567, with their patented electric switches. The Windsor Arcade, marvel of the new century, only lasted ten years, but did make this book's cover.

FIFTH & W 43RD: Young's Hats (1) at no. 504 is seen in a time when everyone wore a hat; on sale at Young's, a hat would be $5 (inflated today upward to $150). Huyler's Candies (2), at no. 508 (est. 1874), grew to fifty-four stores. It hired Milton S. Hershey as an apprentice in 1883 until 1885; he returned to Pennsylvania to establish his own business and the Hershey Bar. Alice Maynard Women's Wear, at no. 510, was next to Guaranty Trust, at no. 512, on the W 43rd St. corner, which is now an architectural glass cube. While the northwest corner teardown was previously Edourd the tailor and above Maison Maurice the milliner, at no. 516. Next door, at no. 518, a lady could get discrete service (3) at Madame Irene, selling corsets. Henri Bendel, gowns and millinery, at no. 520 was exalted by Cole Porter's "You're the Top"; "♪You're a 'Bendel Bonnet' a Shakespeare sonnet; You're Mickey Mouse.♪" Bendel also introduced Coco Chanel (4) to America with her fragrance #5. The large building at the far end of the block (no. 522) was Sherry's Restaurant; in 1898, it faced off with Delmonico's on the east and west corners of Fifth and 44th as they vied to win the favor of Mrs. Astor's elite society. Delmonico's may have had their famous steak, but Louis Sherry offered his show-stopping "dinner on horseback" in one of his private dining rooms on the fourth floor (5); this saw thirty-six guests provided with trays of food attached to saddles and champagne sipped through a saddle bag straw.

FIFTH & W 45TH TO 46TH: Actress Lillie Langtry (1), sweetheart from touring the Golden West, would shop for hats from Lichtenstein, at no. 540, and fine gems set in silver from Marcus & Co. (2), at no. 544, and perhaps a gown from Mary Anderson Warner on the southwest corner of 45th. On the northwest corner was Silo's Fifth Avenue Art Galleries at no. 546, one of several locations founded in 1879 by James P. Silo (3). The Christie's of his day, he auctioned off the contents of many of the Fifth Avenue mansion ahead of the wrecking ball. A floor above Silo's was A. Roman, ladies tailored riding habits as modeled by equestrian, Vera Morris (4). Above Madame M. Obry's at no. 548 was the fine art of Louis Ralston's gallery, now connected with the National Gallery, D.C. L.P. Hollander & Co. (nos. 550–552) offered multiple floors of women's and children's clothes (5). All those store fronts would come down for office buildings with nos. 554, 556, and 558 surviving.

FIFTH & W 46TH: Louise G. Thompson of Louise & Co. (no. 544), one of several dressmakers on the avenue, was also known for her bonnets as she applied for trademark status in January 1888 and remained serving Fifth Avenue for more than twenty-five years, especially during Easter. Above was art dealer M. Knoedler & Co. (no. 556); another location was under construction/conversion from its former mansion days. Next door, at no. 556, was the jewelry salon (2) of Jacob Dreicer (3) & Son, patronized by First Lady Ida McKinley, seen wearing a J. Dreicer tiara (4). Charles Thorley moved his florist business (est. 1871) up to no. 562 Fifth Avenue in 1909; this was the former five-story mansion of Caroline S. Harper. He planted cascading plants—a French touch—from every window; over the years, the "House of Flowers" caught the eye of thousands who passed by (5) before it was torn down. Beyond was J. M. Gidding & Co. (no. 564) for imported women's apparel, a second Fifth Avenue location for Pickslay Fine Jewelry (no. 570), and Samuel Budd's haberdasher (6) (no. 572).

FIFTH & W 47TH: Exclusive homes were either razed or remodeled to house retail businesses, as was Budd & Co. Haberdashery (est. 1861) at Fifth and 24th as they built their second store on Fifth up here at no. 572 (1). Next door at no. 574, the Chevalier row-mansion had gone retail in 1903 as Udall and Ballau, Jewelers (2). The imposing five-columned façade of Howard & Co. was a favorite of First Lady Helen Taft (3) for her jewel selections. Now known as the "Diamond District" and noted by oversized gem-illuminations, Mrs. Taft might have crossed W 47th to no. 580, and the old-world art (4) of the Goldschmidt Gallery or to Miss Carroll's Gowns at no. 582. The last holdout mansion on the block, no. 584, belonged to retired woolen merchant Arthur T. Sullivan, but his son, Leonard (5), would sell after his death. Peck & Peck's hosiery workroom (6) at no. 588 was next to Scott & Fowles, art dealers, at no. 590, at the W 48th Street corner.

FIFTH & W 49TH: Margaret Olivia Slocum Sage (1), a.k.a. the beloved "Old Maid" Widow, at no. 604, philanthropically spread her sizable wealth around in her platonic husband Russell Sage's name (2). The southwest corner, no. 608, was the Goelet Mansion. Their daughter, Mary, wedded Henry Innes-Ker, 8th duke of Roxburghe, thus bringing a noted "title" into the family. Ogden Goelet, stockholder in the Metro Opera House, held Box no. 1; his wealth from real estate ironically spent his last five years living aboard his favorite yacht, the *Norseman* (4). NW 49th at no. 610 was the John R. Kane mansion, becoming by 1933 the French Consulate (5); today, it is the Libraire de France. Further up the block, Gen. Daniel Butterfield (6) at no. 616, now the address serving as the plaza to 30 Rock and the annual Christmas tree. Butterfield was chief of staff and orchestrator of Civil War's Gen. Hooker, who provided prostitutes to keep his licentious troops happy, hence, credit due, today's ladies of the night being referred to as "hookers." Butterfield's father also co-founded American Express—talk about credit due: "Don't leave home without it!"

FIFTH & W 51ST: Dean's Caterers (1), the awning at no. 628, was centrally positioned to serve the number of mansions on Fifth Avenue, not to a mention horse and wagons, this one no. 8, to deliver. There was no connection with Dean and Deluca (est. 1977) in Soho. Next door at no. 632 was Joseph Importers; then there was a vacant lot at no. 634, about where today "Atlas" now holds the weight of the world. On the other side of the lot, at no. 636, were the experts and dealers in old English silver, Crichton Bros. of London (2). Sharing the building that was on the southwest corner of 51st was Gimpel and Wildenstein Works of Art, at no. 638. The Wildenstein family, with a list of Fifth Avenue clients, had their skeletons of scandal, illuminated by Hector Feliciano's 1997 book *The Lost Museum*, dealing with art brokers during WWII buying and selling art the Nazis plundered from Jews. Ironic as it was, the Gimpel's son, Rene A. Gimpel, also a member of the Louis Vuitton family and author of *Diary of an Art Dealer* (3), would die at Neuengamme concentration camp. The northwest corner was one of the Vanderbilt houses, rented to Henry Clay Frick (4) between 1905 and 1915. Frick, an American industrialist and union buster, would later build the historic Frick Mansion further up Fifth Avenue, now a landmark museum for his art collection.

FIFTH & E 49TH: The Hotel Buckingham (1), no. 621 at the southeast corner at 50th (1890–1924), was next door to no. 617, the Democratic Club (2), noted by the flag pole over the front door. Kennedy Galleries (the awning at no. 613, est. 1874), was founded by Hermann Wunderlich, going through several partner and name changes to remain the oldest art gallery in America, fulfilling the décor of the day—millionaire status of overloaded walls of art. On the northwest 49th Street corner was the Belgravia apartments. The block would be bought, razed, and become Saks Fifth Avenue (3), commandeering changes in 1924 while noting the centennial of the avenue. Miss E. H. White was at no. 609; in a matching mansion at no. 607 of Mrs. C. H. Gardner was the private Gardner School for Girls, a Baptist ministry (est. 1860); just beyond the panorama at nos. 603 and 601 were additional five-story city manors (4).

FIFTH & E 51ST: The corner at E 52nd, once a Catholic orphan asylum (no. 653), was the newly constructed mansion (1) c. 1905 of Morton Plant. His beloved new thirty-one-year-old wife, Maisie, had her heart set on a $1 million set of pearls, so Morton (2) made a trade with Cartier (mansion for pearls) and commissioned this portrait (3). In true theatrical serendipity, this author had gone to this Cartier and got his matching tri-gold-ring wedding bands (a.k.a. the Trinity ring), popularly featured in the 1990s. Next door, at nos. 645 and 647, twin limestone mansions built by George W. Vanderbilt was immediately leased by art collector Robert Goelet (4), (brother of Ogden Goelet) and William B. O. Field to accommodate his mother, Augusta, and sister, Mary, both seen here (5). At E 51st corner was the Union League Club (6), with very exclusive membership, although club affiliate Bruce Ismay (7), executive of White Star Line on the *Titanic*, abandoned his fellows by slipping into a lifeboat disguised as a woman. The club was built in 1876 just ahead of the completion of St. Patrick's Cathedral (8). The cathedral was quite the twenty-year project, commencing on the grounds of a Jesuit college and designated cemetery in 1858, interrupted by the Civil War, and completed in 1878.

FIFTH & W 51ST TO 52ND TO 53RD: The Triple Palaces (1) were built in 1882 (nos. 640, 642, and around the corner at no. 2 W 52nd) by William Henry Vanderbilt (2) for his three daughters. On the northwest corner, the Petit Chateau at no. 660 (3) was also built in 1882 for William Henry's son, William K. Vanderbilt (4) and his wife, Alva. She would design it and then throw a $3-million, 1,000-guest housewarming. They bought and then razed the neighboring brownstone next door, no. 666, for their son, William K., Jr., and a conforming six-story mansion was constructed in 1905. Both mansions would come down and be replaced with a forty-story building in 1957. Eventually, the address, no. 666, would become a bad omen with the Kushner's questionable acquisition decisions—first overpaying $1.8 billion, the highest amount on Fifth Avenue for that forty-floor height, then, perhaps with international loan notes coming due, a rumored projected fiscal replacement plan with an eighty-story shops/office/condos complex, including another $4 billion construction loan. The southwest corner, no. 670, was the Brewster & Co. automobile and carriage purveyors (est. 1810 to 1937). The carriage customer list included the Vanderbilts and other prominent Fifth Avenue families. Brewster easily made the transition to electric cars in 1896 and the Rolls-Royce by 1914. On the northwest corner, above in 1911, the St. Thomas Episcopal Church being rebuilt after a fire had destroyed the taller steeple (as seen in 6). Originally opening in 1870, the wealthy parish began an Easter Day tradition, after services, proceeding to nearby St. Luke's Hospital bearing food and presents for the needy while dressed in festive bonnets; it continues today as the "Easter Parade."

FIFTH & W 55TH TO 56TH: Following the larger building trend startup in 1901 of John J. Astor's St. Regis hotel, across the street, the Gotham Hotel at no. 700 rose to eighteen stories in 1905. Part of the Peninsula Hotel group since 1988, the entrance (1) remains the same as in 1938 when traffic stopped with 10,000 gawkers on Fifth as a young man, John Warde (2), on the seventeenth floor pondered "the leap"; his sister persuaded him to come inside, but a press photographer's flash sent him off the ledge, down to that awning. The 1951 film version, *Fourteen Hours*, had a happier ending. The Fifth Avenue Presbyterian Church (est. 1808 in lower Manhattan), following parishioners' trends, relocated up to the northwest corner at 55th, under construction by 1875 (3). Noted both for its cavernous interior (4), and with the advent of the telephone, the church had come up with "Dial-A-Prayer." Cartier, at no. 714, had their original location next door, a little jewel-box of a store; no. 716, Schumann & Co. (5), got the overflow, but eventually upgraded to match the height of all the other storefronts. On the end corner, Harry Winston, one-time owner of the Hope Diamond, sparkled with his jewelry at no. 716 since the 1930s.

FIFTH & E 53RD: Charles W. Harkness (1), at no. 685, the son of Stephen Harkness, an original investor of Standard Oil, inherited and became the second-largest stockholder right behind the Rockefeller family. Although quite irresponsible in his Yale days, he became quite philanthropic. Two doors down at no. 681 was the home of Levi Morton (2), the twenty-second vice president of the United States (1889–1893), who was integral in Statue of Liberty arrangements; he also served a short term as governor of New York. Between Chas and Levi's houses was the Criterion Club, purchasing in 1903 the Newcomb Mansion at no. 683; they tore it down and erected a six-story edifice with a two-story, four marble column entry; it was a prestigious Jewish men's organization, thus avoiding the Christian-only restricted clubs. Cornelius Vanderbilt III (3), buying no. 677 in 1904, became the black sheep of the family because of his choice of bride and he was only left $1.5 million in his father's will compared to his brother's $42 million. Regardless, he eventually rose to the rank of brigadier general during WWI. Attorney Samuel Untermyer was at no. 675, and his neighbor was the "pear soap king," James Pyle at no. 673. Above, his automobile is out front of his soon-to-be-razed home, going commercial modern in 1911 (4), and so began that block changeover. At no. 665 was the Schieffelin family home. The Schieffelin daughter, Margret (6), seems a bit jovial at the Bethesda Fountain, perhaps because the family fortune was founded in pharmaceutical in the late 1700s. Plus during twentieth-century Prohibition loopholes, a shift from drugs to alcohol intended for medicinal purposes, hence prescribing Hennessy Cognac and Moët & Chandon Champagne, produced a business boom.

FIFTH & E 55TH: Among all the Vanderbilt mansions on Fifth Avenue ironically lived Francis de R. Wissman, at no. 707, the city tax assessor, while next door, at no. 705, newly arrived from Europe dealing with family partnership intrigue was art expert Jacques Seligman (1), dealing in impressionism but introducing modern art—such as Picasso's *Les Demoiselles d'Avignon* (1907) (2), sold to the Museum of Modern Art in 1937. Above and around on E 55th, also dealing art on both sides of the Atlantic was Eugene Glaenzer (3) from 1880 to 1940. He had the foresight to mount a large but classy stone-signage gallery plaque facing the entrance of John Jacob Astor's new (1904) twenty-story St. Regis Hotel (4), named for a popular lake resort in the Adirondacks. Fine dining (5) became the place to be seen, and gallery walks after became a Fifth Avenue tradition. Today, a walk would be making impulsive jewelry purchases from new St. Regis in-house location of Harry Winston or nearby Cartier. Mr. and Mrs. Brewster (6) are seen here on a Fifth Avenue carriage ride, likely diners as they lived very nearby—next door at no. 695; on the other side, at no. 693, was W. Kirkpatrick Brice (7), handsome son of U.S. Senator Calvin Brice (Ohio) and treasurer of the NYC Community Chorus.

FIFTH & E 57TH: Just past the Plaza Bank at the southeast corner of 58th at no. 745 was the home of William E. Iselin (1) of the prominent New York family of bankers, merchants, and yachtsmen. Next door, at no. 743, was Robert Guggenheim (2) and his wife, Irene Rothschild, known for their philanthropic art foundation and that museum up at Fifth and 89th. At no. 741 street level was the gallery of art importer Frank Partridge, who had survived the sinking of the torpedoed *Lusitania* on May 7, 1915, drawing the U.S. into WWI. On his crossing, although traveling associates mocked him, he sat up nightly on deck wearing a life jacket (3), hence he was saved while others slept in their cabins as they went down with the ship. Above his shop was the home of Dorothy Arnold (4), who on December 12, 1910, impeccably dressed with a black fox muff, walked out of her home, bought ½ a pound of chocolates, ran into a friend at Brentano's (on Fifth & 27th), and vanished. Family cosmetic business wealth and a U.S. Supreme Court Justice uncle did not buy any results but did change the way police handled disappearances. On the northeast corner was Mrs. Herman Oelrich's mansion (5), whose wealth was from the Comstock gold rush and rebuilding San Francisco after the 1906 quake. A loveless marriage, it positioned her well as the grand dame in society as she married off her sister, Birdie, to the boy across the street, Wm. K. Vanderbilt II. On the southeast corner, now Tiffany's, was the home of Collis P. Huntington (6) and wife, Arabella (7). Ruthless in railroad and politics, he succumbed in 1900, leaving her to marry his nephew, Henry E. Huntington (8) of the Huntington Library in California; she would become legally "Arabella Huntington Huntington." No. 721 was the home of Charles W. Morse, convicted twice of Tammany Hall's sleazy price gouging of the city, but paled by the perpetrated con of twice-impeached president, connected with that current address tag, Trump Towers, bringing constant picketers to Fifth Avenue. In between, No. 721 was the peaceful location of Bonwits Teller department store until torn down.

FIFTH & E 59TH: The Savoy Hotel was originally built in 1890 (1) across from the taller Netherlands Hotel, and seen again in a postcard (2) spanning the block. Harry S. Black, owner of the Plaza Hotel directly across the plaza, would eventually buy the Savoy and leveled that entire block in 1927 to build the new thirty-three-story "Savoy" (3). Hilton's 1958 acquisition would rebrand the Savoy Hilton while around the corner at no. 7, E 58th, the new home for Trader Vic's (4) was built. Claiming to be the originator of specialty "umbrella" cocktails, Vic's replaced the then tired Red Coach Inn. The Savoy-Plaza's name change again in 1964, for the hoopla of the NY World's Fair, was short-lived; the following year, the whole block was razed to make way for the forty-eight-story Eastern headquarters of General Motors, with a ground floor showroom set for the 1968 GM models. Today, it is the home of the glass cube Apple Store. Across 58th was the Plaza Bank, at no. 759, (5), seen being built as a mansion in 1860. Above the bank, within the Mansard roof, was the studio of famous portrait photographer Dudley Hoyt.

FIFTH & W 58TH: In addition to a summerhouse, called the "Breakers" in Newport, RI, Cornelius Vanderbilt II and his wife, Alice (1) had the largest mansion (seen above) in New York State, covering nos. 742–746 Fifth Avenue. Using a bit of his inheritance from family wealth through shipping, railroad, and real estate, they tore down eight brownstones and built the 130 rooms. Seen from the back on 57th (2) is the entrance they always used, leaving the front facing the plaza on 58th for more formal receptions (3), impressing guests with incredible art-covered walls (4). After he died in 1899, Alice remained until she sold the property in 1926 to a commercial developer's wrecking ball (5); it soon became (below) Bergdorf Goodman. The "Dynasty of Fifth Avenue" was the Vanderbilt children: William (Bill) died at twenty-one in the mansion's upper floor of typhoid. Alfred lost his life aboard the doomed sinking of the *Lusitania*. Gladys became a countess via her marriage to Count László Széchenyi. Gertrude Vanderbilt Whitney was a bit of a "flapper." Reginald C. Vanderbilt's wife, Gloria Morgan, gave birth to their daughter, the last noted Vanderbilt, Gloria Vanderbilt. Little Gloria would become a Fifth Avenue debutant/entrepreneur and mother of well-respected reporter Anderson Cooper.

Vanderbilt Family of Fifth Avenue

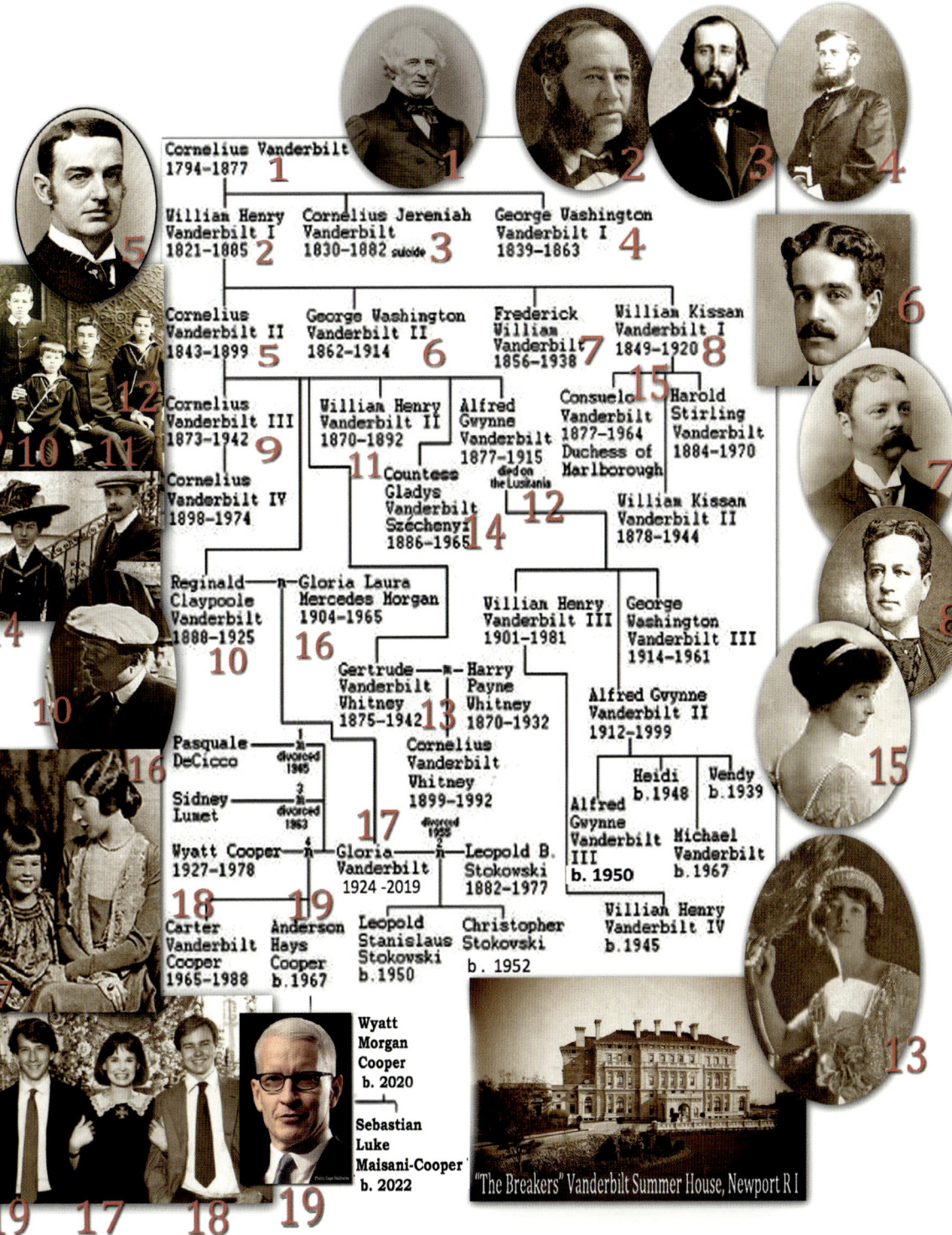

Fifth & 58th: Another victory arch on Fifth Avenue was commissioned in 1893 for the site next to the Vanderbilt mansion, fronting the "Grand Army Plaza" that was just north of 59th. Finally completed in 1900, it was short-lived with arguments that it was dwarfed by the twelve-story Savoy, the fifteen-story New Netherland Hotel, and the plaza itself, along with the objections of the Vanderbilts. Its fate was to be moved to Riverside Park, then by 1902 again to W 89th Street, being revamped to fit the surrounding park. If left in the original Fifth and 58th location, it would have been a bit of bottleneck when the avenue south of Central Park was widened in 1908 as below. Two-way traffic ended in 1966.

FIFTH & W 59TH: The Plaza Hotels: A fashionably private New York Skating Club (1) occupied the block since 1863, but in twenty years, it would become the eight-story construction site of the first Plaza Hotel (2). Therefore, incorporating the plan of a new ice rink just across the street in the new Central Park was a "must," and finally it would be rebuilt and remain as the 1950 Wollman's Rink. By 1905, keeping up with the Savoy and the Netherlands Hotels going up across the plaza, the eight-story Plaza would be torn down, and the twenty-one-story replacement (3) that Manhattanites have come to know would replace it by 1907. Today, as folks emerge from the subterranean Apple store's glass-cubed lobby, where once stood the Savoy, they can catch one of the cabriolets designed *c.* 1834 by Joseph Hansom. The carriages are still perfect for a romantic park ride; catch one parading in front of the Plaza Hotel (4), a structure seemingly enclosed in glass as a jewel. It is quite a mix of centuries that seem to be the hallmark of Manhattan.

69

FIFTH & 59TH: Surrounded by the Netherlands Hotel, the Savoy Hotel, the Vanderbilt estate, the Plaza Hotel, and the entrance through Scholar's Gate to Central Park is the Grand Army Plaza (of the Potomac) above/left in the 1920s. Always planned as an urban gathering place as on the right in Victorian times, it was completed by 1916, to be named in 1923. The center of the northern half of the plaza is the rather gold equestrian statue of William Tecumseh Sherman. On the southern half in front of the Vanderbilt Mansion and the Plaza Hotel is the Pulitzer Fountain. Newspaperman and labeled yellow journalist Joseph Pulitzer's dying bequest of $50,000 was to ensure the fount-tribute. Today, it is still an urban gathering place with several art installations included. Around the Pulitzer Fountain, back in 2011, was Ai Weiwei's *Circle of Animals* based on the zodiac. New York added to the exhibit tour that includes Taipei, Paris, Jackson Hole, Los Angeles, and Toronto. (*zodiacheads.com*)

FIFTH & 59TH: Through the Scholar's Gate and into Central Park to the left is the Gapstow bridge. Curving gracefully over the inlet of the pond at Fifth Avenue and 59th Street was the first bridge seen here in 1895, a bit more elaborate in wood and iron, designed by Jacob Wrey Mould (left corner), who, among other park visual joys, planned the Bethesda Fountain. Originally built in 1874, its constant deterioration from the elements necessitated the change in 1896 to one of the iconic bridges, a.k.a. the other 59th Street bridge. Central Park's romantic setting, as on this snowy night in the twenty-first century, one of the twelve most popular wedding picture sites in the park.

FIFTH & E 60TH: On the northeast corner of Fifth and 60th across from the park entrance was the elite private social Metropolitan Club, for the who's who of Fifth Avenue. It was formed by J. P. Morgan (1) in 1891 with Stanford White designs for the acquired land of the duchess of Marlborough (2), a.k.a. the daughter of Cornelius Vanderbilt II. Across 60th was the Madison Trust Co., sporting its distinctive four-faced sidewalk clock archway (3). Next door at no. 785 was one of eight Park and Tilford grocers, selling fine liquor and imported cigars, which was convenient for next door, the seventeen-story, Wm. Waldorf Astor-owned, New Netherlander Hotel (4): the tallest hotel in the world, state of the art for 1882 with telephones in every room, rebuilt in 1927. Its unusual guests included, seen here in their rooms, Flo Ziegfeld's French chanteuse Anna Held (5)—not known for her talent as a singer but more for the 40 gallon-a-day milk baths (at 20 cents a gallon) and the resulting unpaid bill of $64 to a Long Island milk merchant. Miss Held (6) claimed that the milk was not fresh enough—all pretty much for publicity attributed to Ziggy, an expert in public relations and discoverer of "funny girl" Fanny Brice, Eddie Cantor, and Will Rogers for his Ziegfeld "Follies" (7); lest we forget his start at the 1893 World's Fair, a promo of the first beefcake, Standow (8). Milk baths aside, the Ziegfelds declared their non-clergy/non-public marriage, with witnesses being "Diamond Jim" Brady and Lillian Russell. His second marriage was to actress Billie Burke, a.k.a. Glenda the Good Witch from Oz.

FIFTH & E 61ST: The northeast corner of 62nd at no. 810 was the home of Mrs. Amsinck, crossing 62nd to the southeast corner at no. 807; it was befitting in grand style, the home of Josephine Schmidt, a.k.a. Don Giovanni del Prado (1), ultimately selling to the Knickerbocker Club for their new home relocating from the Fifth and 32nd location. Mrs. William L. Bull lived at no. 805 and William E. Roosevelt (the Oyster Bay, Teddy Roosevelt branch) at no. 804. For William Ellis Corey (2), president of Carnegie Steel and U.S. Steel, and much like the freighter *William E. Corey* named for him, turbulent waters were ahead. He got a "quickie" Reno divorce and the social scandal that went with it, marrying his longtime lover, Broadway star Mabelle Gillman (3); then as a wedding gift, he bought her a mansion further up Fifth. The northeast corner of 61st at nos. 802–03 was the home of Albert and Maria Stokes Bostwick (4) and their five children, with Mother adjusting wee baby Lillian's costume, *c.* 1910 (5). Like their father who set several auto speed records, they would all grow to become accomplished horseman or, in daughter Dorothy Bostwick's case, an accomplished aviatrix. On the southeast corner was the home of Elbridge T. Gerry (6); his manor (7) was constructed in 1895 (note the construction shake in 4).

FIFTH & E 63RD: The extreme left was the home of Clifford V. Brokaw (no. 825), but one might surmise that his heart resided several blocks west at the 79th Street mooring of many of the yachts of Fifth Avenue including his, the *Sybarita* (1). Next door at no. 824 was the prominent social figure James P. Kernochan (2), whose life was cut short at Fifth and 41st on March 6, 1897, when he was struck down by a trap, a popular light, sporty, two-wheeled horse-drawn carriage driven by the charming debutante Grace Baker, daughter of George Baker, bank president and another prominent social figure. Across 63rd was the home of businessman/racehorse owner Robert L. Gerry. Along with his brother, Peter, a U.S. senator, they were the great grandsons of Elbridge Gerry (3), fifth vice president and signer of the Declaration of Independence. Elbridge was also the namesake of the term "gerrymandering," a duplicitous process of redrawing electoral districts to aid the political party in power generally favoring the rich. Frederic Baker (no. 815) built his home in 1871 next to Thomas Rutter (no. 814), president of the NY Central RR, and George McMurty (no. 812), president of American Sheet Steel Co., who had by 1895 built his own 640-acre company enclave (4) in Vandergrift, Pa. Frances L. Loring (no. 811) of Aetna Real Estate & Loan, and NY landscape artist William Belden (no. 810) built their mansions by 1885 and joined the block's fight against City Hall, demanding the Central Park's zoo across the street be removed (5); the animals were polluting the soil and the aroma was polluting their garden parties. By the 1940s, the mansions were replaced with these high-rise apartment houses, meaning no more backyard garden parties, so the lions, tigers, bears and elephants were spared.

FIFTH & E 65TH: The home of publisher J. P. Morton (no. 844), built in 1870 (1), was updated in 1907. But quite impressive was his neighbor at 840 Fifth, corner of 65th Street—John Jacob Astor IV (2) and his eighteen-year-old expectant bride, Madeleine (3). They produced avenue gossip that went silent with word of the sinking of the *Titanic* as the honeymooning couple were aboard. She survived but the richest man on board went down with the ship. His body, one of only a few recovered, was reduced to this description: "#124-male-est. age 50-light hair & moustache," followed by list of effects and cash on him, ending with: "FIRST CLASS. NAME: J.J. ASTOR IV." Today, that house of sorrow is now the Temple Emanu-El. Across 65th, at no. 838, was the home of Wm. Watts Sherman (4), belonging to several patriotic and hereditary societies, while his second wife, Sophia A. Brown (5), was the granddaughter of John Carter Brown, Jr., namesake of Brown University. Isidor Wormser (6) made most of his wealth from California interests parlaying it into New York banking and the stock exchange, dying quietly at home, #836, cause of death simply listed "old age." The last house on the right (no. 834) was that of Frank Jay Gould, seen here (7) walking down Fifth with one of his three wives. He was a French Riviera casino/hotel owner and philanthropist as well as son of Jay Gould.

FIFTH & W 66TH: Central Park Literary Walk Promenade: Along with all of Manhattan, the Fifth Avenue mansions really made use of the promenade that ran from about 66th to 72nd Streets to the band shell and the Bethesda terrace. Designed to draw in a park visitor, the Fifth Avenue and 59th Street corner entrance, known as Scholar's Gate, does just that; past the pond, past the zoo, crossing over 65th, is the Promenade (the Mall). The park has been enjoyed (above in 1902), and since the winter of 1859 with implementation of those changes over the years. The plans submitted by Fredrick Law Olmstead (1) and Calvert Vaux (2) showed a wide, straight path lined with the grand curved branches of American elms as a "Naturalist-palace." The first statue for the "literary walk" was that of William Shakespeare (1), followed by Sir Walter Scott (4), Friz-Green Halleck, and Robert Burns by 1872. The statues were chosen by a committee of actors, including Edwin Booth, brother of assassin, John Wilkes Booth. Popular for nannies with perambulators (5), it was also a favorite of Marlene Dietrich, who would dress up as a nanny and take her grandkids out for an afternoon. It has been rumored that Jackie Kennedy, then the most photo-besieged woman in the world, would sit in her Fifth Avenue high-rise with a telescope spying on Central Parkers. Below is another quiet winter night constitutional.

FIFTH & E 67TH: The house on the extreme left, no. 858, was that of Thomas Ryan (1), who followed the trend and moved uptown from Fifth and 12th neighboring the chateau (2) of railroad and financial magnate, generally considered as one of the Gilded Age Robber barons, Jay Gould (3). Gould built his house in 1868 at the northeast corner (no. 857) and eventually gave it to his son, George Jay Gould, and his wife, Edith (4) as a wedding gift; the couple tore it down in 1906 to build a larger, five-story mansion facing 67th. Across 67th, past no. 855, was the scandal of the block—third house from the corner at 854 Fifth, home of Benjamin Thaw (5), built in 1905 for $60,000. Becoming the Pittsburgh family's New York enclave, Ben's half-brother, Harry Kendall Thaw (6), drew interest when he murdered famed Fifth Avenue architect Stanford White on the evening of June 25, 1906, at the rooftop theatre of Madison Square Garden. Harry was defending his young wife's honor; the first media star, known professionally as Evelyn Nesbit (7, seen at age sixteen), a popular American chorus girl/artists' model/Gibson Girl/actress. The forty-seven-year-old White allegedly drugged a fourteen-year-old Nesbit and then raped her, leading to what the press dubbed the "Trial of the Century." After one hung jury, Harry was found not guilty by reason of insanity. The motion pictures *The Girl in the Red Velvet Swing* and *Ragtime* portrayed the event. The mansion, with copper Mansard roof and opulent Versailles-style rooms, having survived the high-rise apartment boom, is now the Serbia Permanent Mission to the United Nations and was recently on the market for $50 million. The rest of the block—George Kidd (no. 853) and Oliver Payne (no. 852)— laid low, although Mrs. H. O. Havemeyer (8) on the northeast corner of 66th did anything but, as a wealthy and philanthropic suffragette.

FIFTH & E 69TH: Just past the Lenox Library (1) and the spires of the gothic mansion on the southeast corner of 70th was the home with the tall chimney at no. 883 of John Sloane (2), who, along with his brother, William, turned his father's rug business into one of the greatest commercial enterprises—W. J. Sloane. Next door with the arched entry (no. 881) was the home of merchant Adolph Lewisohn (3), who after meeting Thomas Edison in 1870 invested in undervalued copper mines needed for the new electric light bulbs, thus becoming known as the "Copper King" with dividends by 1890 of $35 million. Quoting that he had enough money, he would be philanthropic, sing tenor for amateur opera, and buy art for donation. E. H. Harriman (4) lived on the northeast corner at 69th (no. 880); his wealth came from buying teetering railroads, reorganizing/renaming them, and selling at a profit, while bringing on commerce scrutiny as president of those railroads. He also sponsored and joined the 1899 scientific expedition with John Muir to catalog the vegetation of the Alaska coastline. His son, Wm. Averell Harriman (5), would become secretary of commerce under Truman; foreign advisor to FDR, Kennedy, and Johnson; and the governor of New York State. On the southeast corner on the other side of the political spectrum at no. 878 was Ogden Mills (6), son of banking wealth and president of the NY State Tax Association; he too would run for governor of New York, but as a Republican. Francis B. Harrison (7), at no. 876, Democratic five-term U.S. congressman, lived next to Daniel Gray Reid (8), at no. 875. Reid had built behind his home a three-story carriage house—the first floor accommodated fourteen automobiles; the second floor, stalls and ramp for his sixteen horses; and the third floor, servants. Neighborly C. F. Stickney (no. 874) never seemed to complain of the expected smells.

FIFTH & E 71ST: Lenox Library: Nathalie Elizabeth Ray Baylies, the young widow at thirty-two of Edmund Lincoln Baylies, carried on his name by building the Baylies Mansion (1) at Fifth and 71st in 1892. The house itself caused a neighborhood ruckus when its bay windows overhung the vacant lot of Mrs. Isabella Sattherthwaite. The costly construction changes infuriated the pearl-clutching Widow Baylies, ending traditions of bay windows on Fifth Avenue mansions, and damaged future social invitations for Mrs. Sattherthwaite. Isabella's lot remained undeveloped for more than twenty years. James Lenox (2) had started this "mansion building boom" when, in 1877, he built his Lenox Library on his long-held family farm. But the boom actually occurred after he died in 1880; the farm was sold off and mansions sprung up along upper Fifth such as Mrs. Baylies'. Lenox, filling his grand reading room (3), also purchased for $2,400 the Gutenberg Bible in 1847, the first major book printed back in the 1450s using movable type, becoming part of the collection. A coach can be seeing coming in along Fifth Avenue (2); today it is a yellow cab.

FIFTH & W 72ND, BETHESDA FOUNTAIN: Across Fifth at 72nd in Central Park, above, was the designer Calvert Vaux and his assistant Jacob Mould's concept for the Bethesda Terrace fountain, with construction starting in 1862 (1). It included the 1868 Emma Stebbins 8-foot neoclassical sculpture, *Angel of the Waters* (2), dedicated in 1873 as the healing waters needed for whatever disease one had, hence its importance in the Kushner play *Angels in America* about the AIDS epidemic. The gondola (3) was gifted by Park Commissioner John Gray in 1862 but without a gondolier. It just floated until the 1890s, when one was found. It was the same gondola until the 1980s, when it was replaced with an authentic Venetian gondola with trained gondoliers—arrange rentals of romantic dreams at the nearby Loeb boathouse.

FIFTH & 73RD: The southeast corner at 74th, opposite the model sailboat pond in Central Park, was undeveloped in 1881, save for a few modest brownstones. William Pickhardt (no. 929) would build—with many changes, teardowns, and restarts—his six-story, ego-driven show of wealth (1), fulfilling a lifelong dream of living on Fifth Avenue. Referred to as "a palace, which is a monument to blighted hopes," it would be bought by Rev. Alfred Pell in 1895, eventually replacing it by 1917 with his own monumental changes—a limestone-clad, twelve-story building with twelve apartments. Some famous twentieth century residents included Mary Tyler Moore, Paula Zahn, and a red-tailed hawk nesting above the twelfth-floor stonework that featured on PBS series *Nature* in c. 2004. The houses that remain there today belonged to John W. Simpson's (2), who had some empty lots (nos. 1026 and 1027) further up Fifth but chose no. 926 for his home (3). H. L. Terrell lived at no. 925. George H. Warren II, real estate developer, whose company founded and owned the Metropolitan Opera, lived next door, at no. 924. His daughter, Constance, a sculptress, would marry Count Guy de Lasteyrie (4) down the block at St Patrick's. The white marble neo-classic style mansion at no. 923 was that of R. Guggenheimer (5); one of his pleasures was to give an annual dinner for the newsboys of the city. An odd occurrence happened in 1921 when a man came to that front door, introducing himself to the butler as composer Irving Berlin, asking to use the telephone and borrow some money. The police were quickly notified, as was the actual mortified Mr. Berlin. The northeast corner at no. 922 was the home of Nicholas Palmer (6), whose handshake deals not to sell out to apartment trends were forgotten by 1949. Crossing 73rd in 1910, the southeast vacant lot's temp-fence uniquely touted Nabisco's Uneeda Biscuits' (7) first tin packaging. The Samuel Thorne mansion went up on the lot at no. 914, with a grand parlor (8) to display (seemingly a status symbol on Fifth Avenue) a woodwind pipe organ.

FIFTH & E 76TH: Temple Beth-El (House of God) was built in the Romanesque style in 1891, with an oversized Moorish dome; it would accommodate 2,900 people, illuminated by the latest 1,000 incandescent bulbs (1). Sadly, all was leveled in 1929 to accommodate this apartment house below, far left. Next door at the northeast corner of 75th Street was the five-story home (which still remains at no. 933) of Edward Stephen Harkness (2), who with Standard Oil investments, made *Forbes Magazine*'s sixth richest man in the U.S in 1918. His wealthy uncle, Lamon Harkness, would endow universities and the Metropolitan Museum of Art. The southeast corner at no. 936 was Edwin Gould (3) and his wife, Sarah (4), thriving quite well with Gould family fortune derived from his father's railroad investments. It also allowed their daughters again to marry noblemen and their sons, consistently, actresses. At no. 934, Alfred M. Hoyt's widow, Rosina, resided in their mansion (5) until her death in 1922. Bought by the bank president of National City Bank (now Citibank) Geo. E. Mitchell, as a teardown, it was replaced with the mansion that exists today. It was sold complete with Mr. Mitchell's furnishings and art for the consulate general of France; all they needed to do was hoist the French flag. Next door at no. 932, Mortimer L. Schiff, president of the Boy Scouts of America, was venerated by a *Scouting* magazine cover (6). In 1907, Schiff's valet, wielding a bowling pin, abruptly assaulted the revered scout master without cause, so the story goes. Unsure of the pin's origin, but little doubt that there would be no merit badge, the valet was discharged.

FIFTH & E 77TH: No. 965 was the home of Jacob H. Schiff (1), influential banker and subject of Naomi W. Cohen's study in American Jewish leadership. Living next door, at no. 963, was Charles F. Dieterich, whose wealth was derived by engineering gasworks—natural gas for home use. Yet the big architectural show at the northeast corner of Fifth and 77th was the former Montana gold and copper miner, trader, and mule driver William A. Clark (2), here with his two daughters from his second marriage to his twenty-three-year-old ward and bride. He parlayed each career move into banking, newspaper and railroads; he was a scandalous U.S. senator for one year, 1899, and the subject of many a cartoon (3). His mansion at no. 952, a.k.a. "Clark's Folly" (1897–1911), had 121 rooms, thirty-one baths (all indoors), four art salons, and a swimming pool—all built via loopholes at a cost of $7 million (today, $180 million). One of Clark's daughters, Huguette, had her own folly in her later years at age eighty-five; she checked into society's Doctor's Hospital, liking the park views, and although she was healthy, she remained for twenty years (at $400,000 *per annum*). She died at 105, never returning to her Fifth Avenue home. No. 955 Fifth was the home of banker/businessman, Horace Harding, with his living room (4) showing off another Aeolian organ (courtesy of Aeolian Co., 1908). Aside from the Harding Hospital (now St. John's Queens), New York commuters recognize the name from the Long Island Expressway; seemingly, the car in front of his mansion is ready to roll. Samuel Willard Bridgham, at no. 954, the grandson of S. W. Bridgham, first mayor of Province, RI, fitting right in, was married to Fanny Schermerhorn (5), the niece of Mrs. Astor, head of NY society.

FIFTH & E 79TH: William and Angeline Curtis (1) in 1906 bought no. 986, with the two rounded bay windows and balustrade balcony, *c.* 1899 (2). Just next door at nos. 984 and 985 was Olympic ice skater Irving Brokaw; here he is ice-skating with his wife in a Central Park pond (3). His father, Isaac Brokaw, at the corner of Fifth and 79th (4), was literary the cornerstone of the four-mansion Brokaw compound. Its proposed landmark status was always stymied until it was too late when, one weekend in February 1965, a surprise demolition cleared the way for a twenty-five-story co-op (at $8 million apiece) with spectacular views. Crossing 79th is the French Gothic chateau, built in 1899 by Isaac D. Fletcher (5). Upon his death in 1917, it was donated to the Met across the street. They kept the artwork but sold the mansion to Sinclair Oil Co.; the founder, Harry F. Sinclair, would end up moving to a jail cell (6) for his corruption during the 1920s Teapot Dome scandal. At no. 972, Oliver Hazard Payne (Standard Oil) had built a Stanford White-designed mansion in 1902 as a wedding gift for his nephew, Payne Whitney, and his bride, Helen Hay, seen here on their wedding day (7). Payne's brother, Harry, wed Gertrude Vanderbilt Whitney, a sculptor, arts patron, and founder of the Whitney Museum. The last of the three houses on the end, no. 971, is the 1912 remodeled home of Henry Cook (8), who since 1879 actually owned the whole block (Fifth and Madison Avenues and 78th and 79th), destined for mansion row as seen down 79th, starting with the corner chateau, below right. He had originally built his own on the northeast corner of Fifth and 78th with his direction and a Stanford White design. Both men would not live to see the home completed—Cook, eighty-three, died in 1905, and White was murdered ten months later.

FIFTH & E 81ST: On the extreme left was the eight-story Beaux-Arts mansion (1) built by the Duke brothers of the American Tobacco Co. (1899–1901). It was retained by the family until 2006, when it was sold for $40 million. James Duke is seen with his daughter Doris Duke (2) along with her glam shot from the Duke University archives (3). Her unhappy life, documented by several films, ended in Beverly Hills in 1993. Most of her $1.2 billion went to her foundations with $5 million and an additional $500,000 *per annum* to her butler, Bernard Lafferty. At the corner of Fifth and 81st, an apartment house is going up in 1911, and below, it remains today. Across the street, a nanny with a perambulator crosses by a vacant lot that waits for another construction start-up. The last two houses on the right are Louis Stern (4) at no. 993 of Stern Bros. department store, who bought in 1884, gave lavishly catered operas with well-appointed guests from the Four Hundred in his drawing room; and at no. 991, in 1918, William Ellis Corey, president of U.S. Steel, having left his wife, purchased it as a wedding gift for his new bride, actress Mabelle Gilman (5). The headlines were "Steel Millionaire Loses Heart to Showgirl." They would divorce in 1923 and Miss Gilman, living in 1940s Paris, would be arrested and interned in a Nazi concentration camp.

Fifth & 81st: On the west side across Fifth surrounded by Central Park is the Metropolitan Museum of Art, first opening in 1872, at no. 681 Fifth. Going through several locations, the museum would open here, no. 1000 Fifth Avenue, in 1902 with ongoing architectural design changes. It was High Victorian Gothic to the left, already dated prior to its completion, which was then fronted by todays Beaux-Arts façade as below before Fifth Avenue was widened, losing the grassy approach and the crescent drive—a good place to catch a hansom cab in those days.

The foyer of the museum, here on the left in 1907 as Statuary Hall, was adapted to receive the ticket-buying public. Originally, there was a nominal admission charge one or more days a week, but that ended in 1940 and New York would proudly proclaim their "public museums" were all free. This remained until in 1970, when an honorary trustee investment banker, ignoring public opinion, pushed a new city lease of Central Park public land to charge a discretionary admission. Back in 1910, the museum had been expanded with added wings on either side of the original structure as seen below, thus becoming the largest museum in the United States and dominating the city's "Museum Mile." Apparently, it is still a good place to catch a cab.

Fifth & E 83rd: Across from the Metropolitan Art Museum, there are a row of houses (*c.* 1903) that are museum pieces themselves. George C. Clark was at no. 1027 (1), and eighty-six-year-old William Kingsland bought no. 1026 for his seventy-eight-year-old bride of over fifty years; poor Will did not survive the move up from Fifth and 17th. Eventually, with donations along with a 1950 purchase of no. 1028, the homes became known as the "3 Graces of Marymount School of NY." The mansion at no. 1025 was that of U.S. representative (NY) Lloyd S. Bryce (2). His neighbor on the corner of 83rd was Richard Arnold, creator of the first department store, but upon his 1889 death and funeral in his mansion, it was closed up for fourteen years until purchased by railroad man, William Solomon, who razed it to go on a six-year building project. Grandeur not withstanding (3), eighteen years later, after his in-mansion funeral, it was razed, this time for an apartment building—another structure built to last 100-plus years surviving less than twenty. The entire vacant block across Fifth and 83rd Street from the new Metropolitan Art Museum would finally be built on in 1905, but just at dead center with somewhat identical mansions including elevators; they were owned by Anthony J. Drexel and his wife, Marjorie Gould (4) at no. 1015, and James Francis Aloysius Clark and his wife Edith, at no. 1014, with large formal dinner parties prevailing at both addresses. The James Gerards (5) would buy no. 1015 in 1919, and by 1926, when the empty lot at no. 1010 became a fifteen-floor apartment house, their neighbor, Clark (6), feeling boxed in, would sell no. 1014 to them. After all, the old Gerard's house was also to come down to make way along with that empty lot for a fourteen-story apartment house. On the upper floors of that building at E 83rd was the home of famed acting coach Stella Adler (7), seen with this author, a friend, who would pay social calls in LA & NY. "Normally stern, and as unbelievable as it sounds, I could bring tears to Stella's eyes singing 'Mama A Rainbow' from the Broadway show, *Minnie's Boys*!"

FIFTH & E 85TH: The mansion at no. 1046 was owned by Michael Dreicer (1), famed family of Fifth Avenue jewelers, who was also financially prosperous by developing the avenue's changeover from mansions to commercial. Like many of his neighbors, when his time was up in 1921, his sizable art collection went to the Met. A year later, his neighbor Lloyd Warren (at no. 1041), founder of the Beaux-Arts Institute of Design, NYC, fell out of his upper story window while sleepwalking (2). James B. Claws (3) built the mansion at the northeast corner at E 85th with his Wall St. money; it was sadly demolished by 1930 along with Warren's home to make way for seventeen stories. The southeast corner was the Fifth Avenue apartments (no. 1038), replaced with a fifteen-story building in 1928. At the end of the block (no. 1034) was Herbert Robbins, wholesale drugs; his house below remains to be another "Mansion sandwich." Herb's neighbor, Countess Annie Leary, used her father's hat business wealth for community patronage, most notably the Christopher Columbus monument that we circumnavigate at Columbus Circle (4). The countess also gave lavish parties in her lavish home (5), filled with sixty-eight lavish and oversized mirrors (she was wild about mirrors). Her title was papal, a testament to her many philanthropies for the church and New York, so when she died in 1919, she was entombed beneath St. Patrick's Cathedral.

89

FIFTH & E 87TH TO 88TH: Extreme left, at no. 1068, was the oversized row house of Leo Stein (1), a great collector of early modern art, who was only matched by his sister, Gertrude Stein (2), who spent most of her time in her Paris salon as a patron of those arts. On the northeast corner of 88th was Henry Phipps and his wife (3), the quiet accountant who in 1901 merged Andrew Carnegie's steel and JP Morgan's steel mills, making its three principal partners—Carnegie, Henry Clay Frick, and Phipps—the richest men in the world. Phipps built here, sparing no expense. Alas, it too, like others, was torn down within twenty years to make way for a 1927 apartment house. The vacant lot across the street, the southeast corner at no. 1058, would be developed in 1914 by James Speyer (4), the third largest Wall Street investment firm, eventually investing in 1951 in the current eighty-seven unit/nineteen stories. Charles P. Pevin was next door, at no. 1056, and two houses over was the home of George Leary, head of Columbia Light, Heat & Power Co., and his wife Mrs. Leary (5). The Learys often entertained social notables at their home, #1053, including of course the Thomas A. Edisons.

FIFTH & E 89TH: Handsome Archer Milton Huntington (1), adopted or rumored biological son of California railroad millionaire Collis P. Huntington, became quite the art patron, having grown up around Collis' art collection and philanthropy as well as his cousin/eventual step-father, Henry E. Huntington (Huntington Library in California). Archer once remarked, "Wherever I put my foot down, a museum springs up." So it is fitting that—across E 89th Street from his home, no. 1083, and neighbor, McLane Igen, the woolen wizard heir at no. 1081—Solomon R. Guggenheim, using some of his mining fortune, would build his museum displaying his vast collection of art. He would purchase William Fuller's home at no. 1072 and the late George Penniman's at no. 1071 (the established address of the museum), and hire Frank Lloyd Wright to design what would be his last project—the Guggenheim Museum; neither Wright nor Guggenheim lived to see its 1959 opening. Here with his daughter (4), Guggenheim with his wife, Irene Rothschild, would also take Peggy Guggenheim under their wing, after her father died on the *Titanic*. With such influences, she became a famed art collector with her own museum in Venice, Italy.

FIFTH & E 91ST: Never did a group of neighborhood urchins have a finer address to play "hoops" (1), albeit temporary, than in this vacant lot at no. 1100, just across the street from Andrew Carnegie, on the corner of Fifth and E 91st. Carnegie purchased his lots in 1898, furthest north of the mansion building boom on Fifth Avenue, to accommodate his wishes for an adjoining garden on its south side (2), as seen here in 1915 after that lot across 91st was built upon. His wealth derived from his steel enterprises. Construction began in 1903 as the first American home with a steel frame as well as a private Otis lift. Extremely philanthropic, he is also known for his 2,509 Carnegie libraries around the country, as illustrated with this 1903 *Puck* cartoon (3). Lest we forget his humanitarian Carnegie Institute, and of course the old joke: "How do you get to Carnegie Hall?" "Practice!"

FIFTH & 93RD: Abruptly, the flurries of "Mansion Mania" on Fifth Avenue seem to end here at 93rd, around 1911. Land investors became billboard backers as traffic did venture further north on the Avenue on their way to the polo grounds to either see the wealthy pursuit of their polo-playing socializing or with some irony the baseball teams of the early 1880s. As the grid of streets were laid out above Central Park, through the grounds in 1889, so baseball moved first up to Washington Height and then to what was touted "The house that [Babe] Ruth built" (1); the New York Yankees (2) and its stadium became a worldwide name. Irony comes when a four-term U.S. congressman, Jacob (Jake) Ruppert, Jr., with family brewery wealth, became the ball team owner (1915-1939). He built his castle (3) at no. 1115, on the corner of 93rd; he bought the contract of Babe Ruth from the Boston Red Sox, which Boston never forgave; then, with his "Ruth" ticket revenue, he built Yankee Stadium. Sharing the block was his neighbor at no. 1109, on the corner of 92nd, was another well-appointed castle, that of Felix Warburg and his wife, Frieda (4). With their delightfully rambunctious five children (one would marry a Rothschild) and thirteen servants to keep the household running, Felix once told his wife "Your Children may be spoiled; mine are fun." Joyously generous, they bequeathed the rare art and furnishings to museums and the house to the Jewish Theological Seminary for their museum. Yet that vacant lot remained until 1925 when billboards came down and much like what would happen to Jake's castle on the southeast corner, they would be replaced with fourteen-story apartment buildings for those who just had to live on Fifth Avenue.

Fifth & 101st Through 104th Street: There were fifteen shacks on Fifth Avenue, just a few blocks north of where those mansions of architectural grandeur, the finest money could buy, had started to thin out past Fifth and 93rd. The carriages and hansom cabs would continue further up the avenue, certainly past here at 101st Street, but their destination was more likely the polo grounds at approximately 111th Street. The middle of that stretch of blocks at 103rd Street would be transformed into the Museum of the City of New York. Established in 1923 to preserve New York's history, it was founded by Henry Collins Brown in 1923 with first exhibits at Gracie Mansion in 1926. A hit with the public, they had to find another location and on city-donated land. Although struggling through cutbacks via the crash on Wall Street, the museum was built between 1929 and 1930 at Fifth and 103rd (nos. 1220–1227), dedicated in 1932, reigning over the block befitting its subject matter—currently 1.5 million items.

FIFTH & 105TH: The front gate at the Vanderbilt Mansion is seen in 1901 at no. 1, 58th Street, at Fifth Avenue. When the house was to be razed in 1927 for Bergdorf's, Alice Vanderbilt had a giant yard sale—perhaps more accurately a giant inside-the-house sale. Somewhat "gutted," several of the mantels and architectural details were incorporated into the New Netherlands Hotel under renovation across Fifth at the corner of 59th Street. However, the famed front gates seen here were donated to the Central Park Conservancy and swing open at Fifth and 105th to the formal gardens beyond, as if going back to "Manderley." Now let's take a Fifth Avenue bus back down to Washington Square.

Acknowledgments

The panorama collection provided by the New York Public Library, "Fifth Avenue From Start to Finish" 1911, was the first tool from which to draw. Detailed yellowed photographs from the archives of the Library of Congress prints and film division were added; the image history collectors are not known. Those who donated their archives, including Pinterest, the Detroit Photo Co., the Metropolitan Museum of Art, with follow-up research with "Wikipedia" is a good *Tales* starting point. Referencing imagery through the Museum of the City of New York and "Fifth Avenue Old and New 1824–1924" helped to flesh out the truth, or at least a "version" of the truth. Much can be found on websites of imaged subjects: Central Park Conservancy, Aeolian Organ, the Vanderbilt archives, and Greenwich Village Society for Historical Preservation.

Contemporary images are those of author/photo-artist Frank Muzzy (with help of hiking boots). Special thanks to Armistead Maupin for sharing his "Tales" titling, Louise Hirschfeld recalling her neighbor, the incomparable Marlene Dietrich, and actor Norman Lloyd (1914–2021) recalling of his Hitchcock "tales." Additional thanks to Gordon Miller for his encouragement and motoring services down Fifth Avenue and, the editing skills of the Fonthill Media staff of Alan Sutton, spotlighting Jamie Hardwick and the PR talents of George Kalchev.

Personally: My reliving memories of a hansom cab ride with a summer romance or a snowy winter stroll through the park and down Fifth Avenue to Rockefeller Center's ice rink of holiday cheer; my first New York gallery exhibit opening in Chelsea, luncheons at the Russian Tea Room, and supper at the Rainbow Room, Top of the Rock, to dance the night away, be it there or a venue in the village.

Appreciation to any Manhattan plot-based film that encouraged dreams of a little lad loving movies and where it took him, a guy relishing walks down Fifth after midnight recalling his own *Tales of Fifth Avenue Through Time*.

I dedicate this work to Ameda Lambert Muzzy, an extraordinary woman, actress, writer, businesswoman, confidante and supporter of all things, and mother—*je t'aime*.

The fifty-sixth floor look of Fifth Avenue from the Rockefeller family offices, showing St. Patrick's Cathedral.